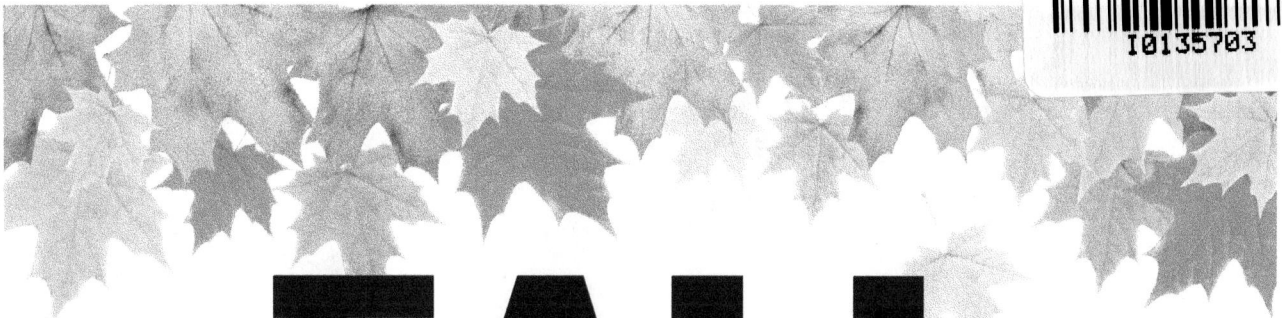

# FALL

# ADULT COLORING

# BOOK

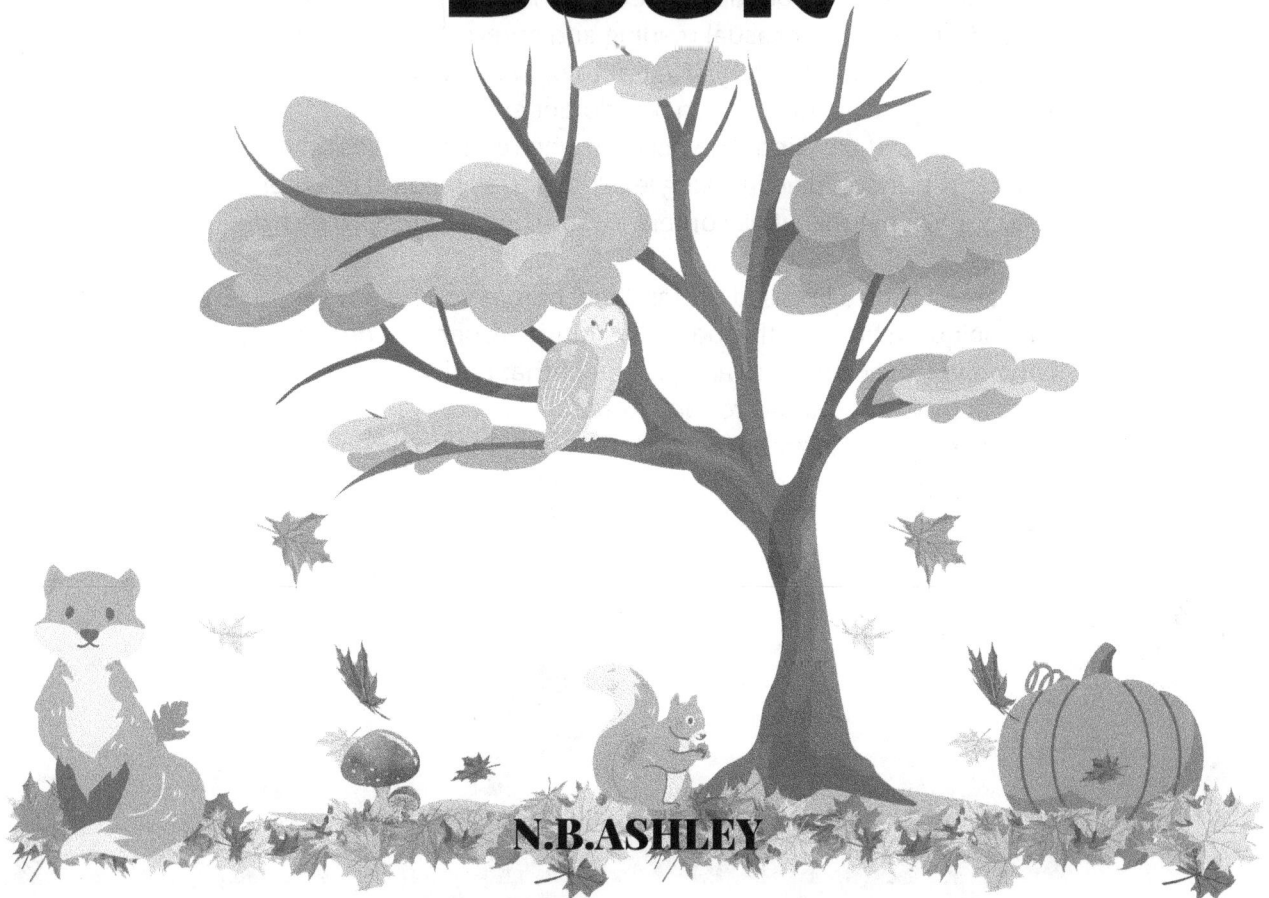

N.B.ASHLEY

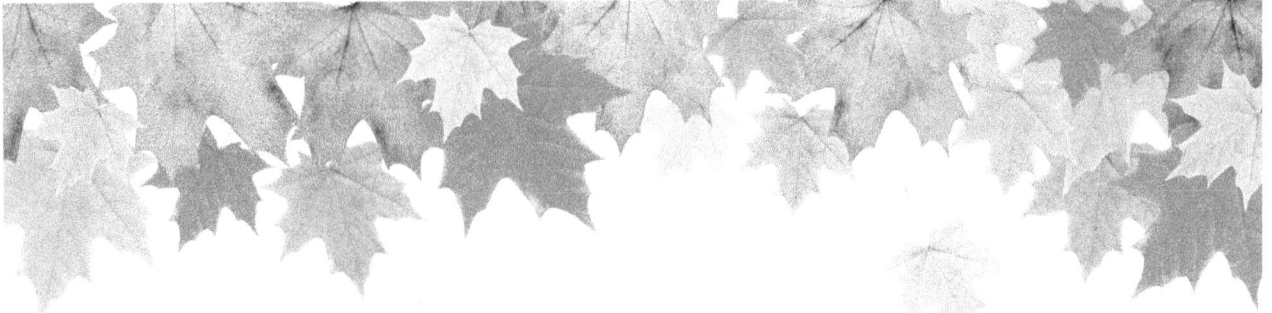

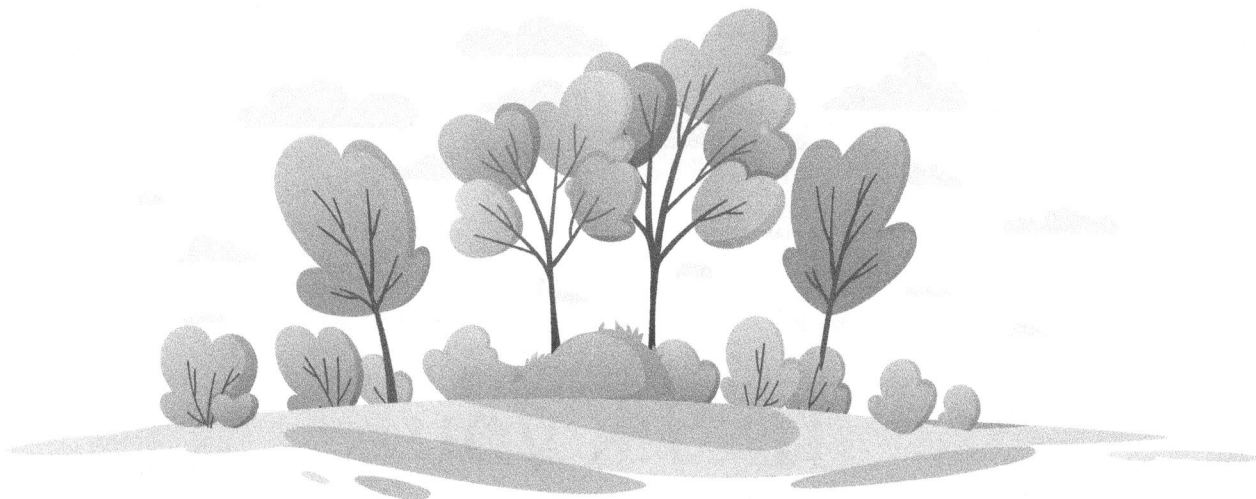

# This Book Belongs to:

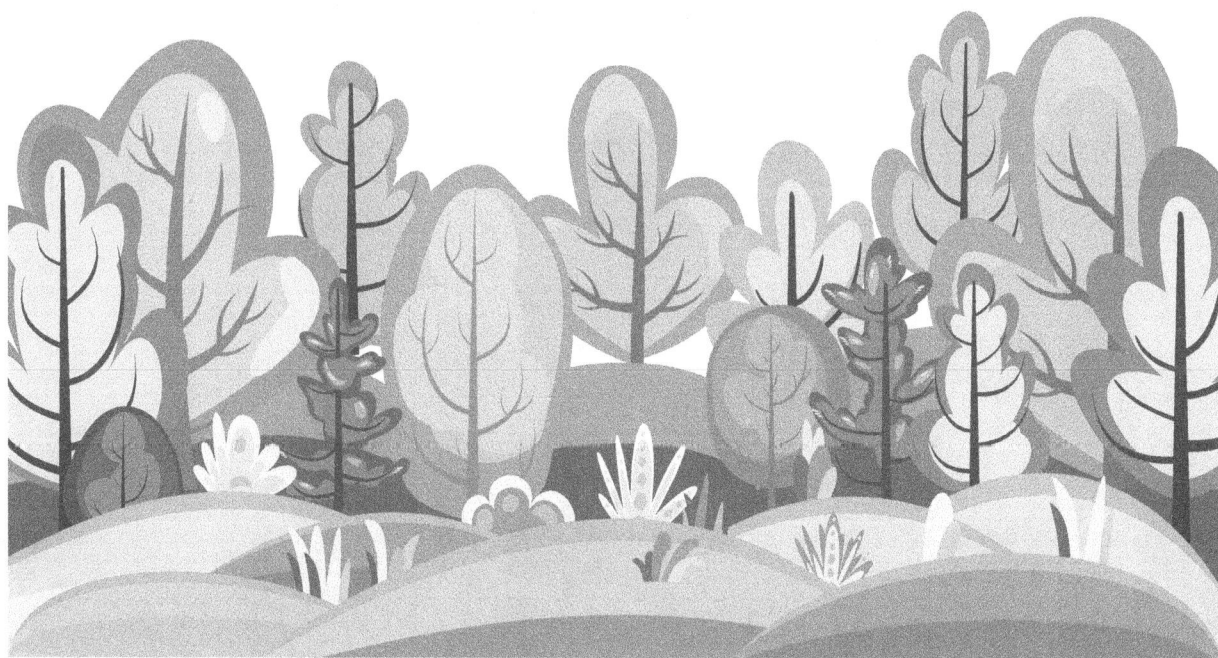

_____
_____
_____

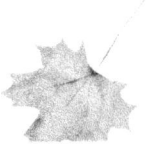
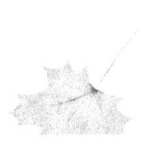

# Thank you

I hope you enjoyed our book.

We would really appreciate your feedback, at the address below:

hello.publish@gmail.com

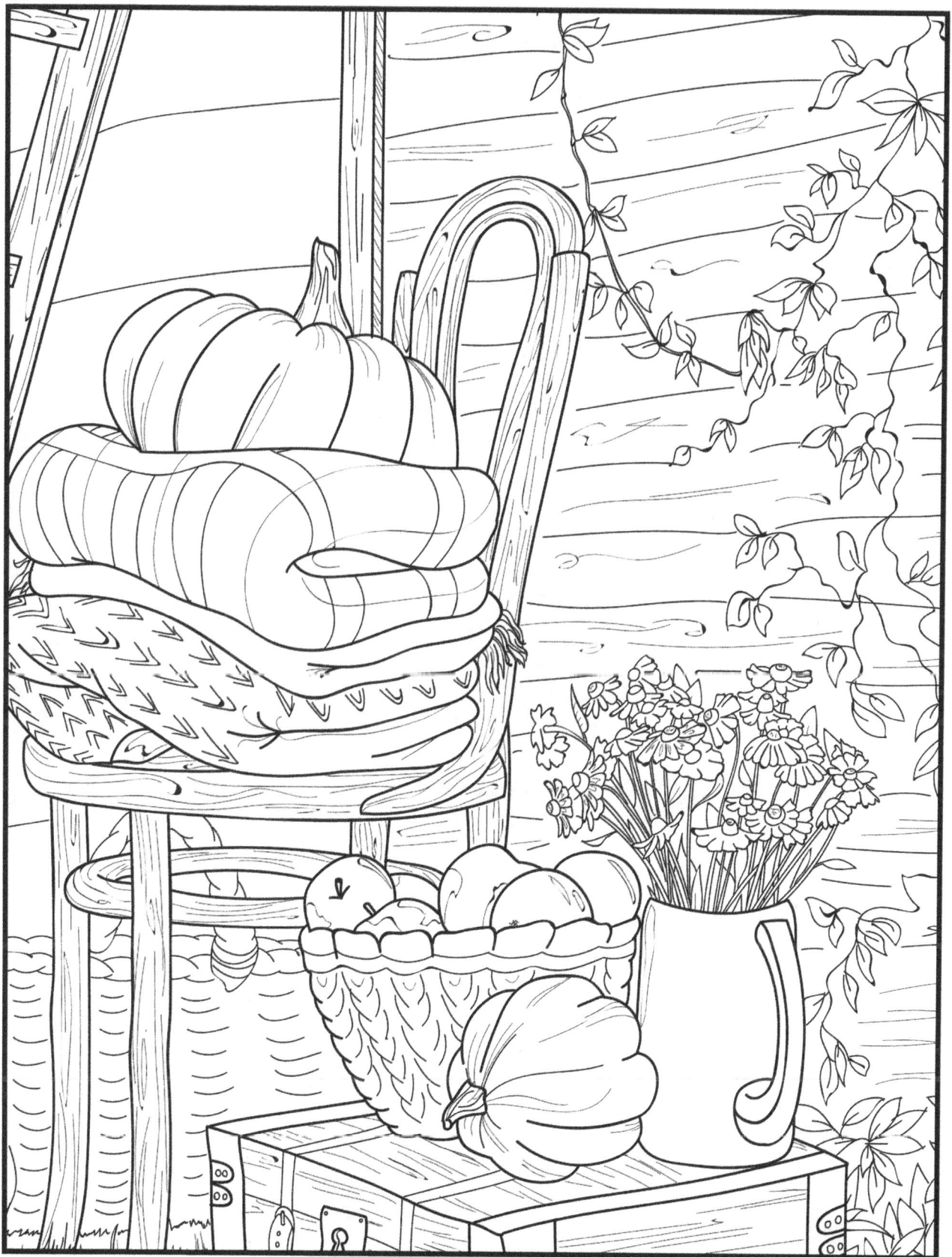

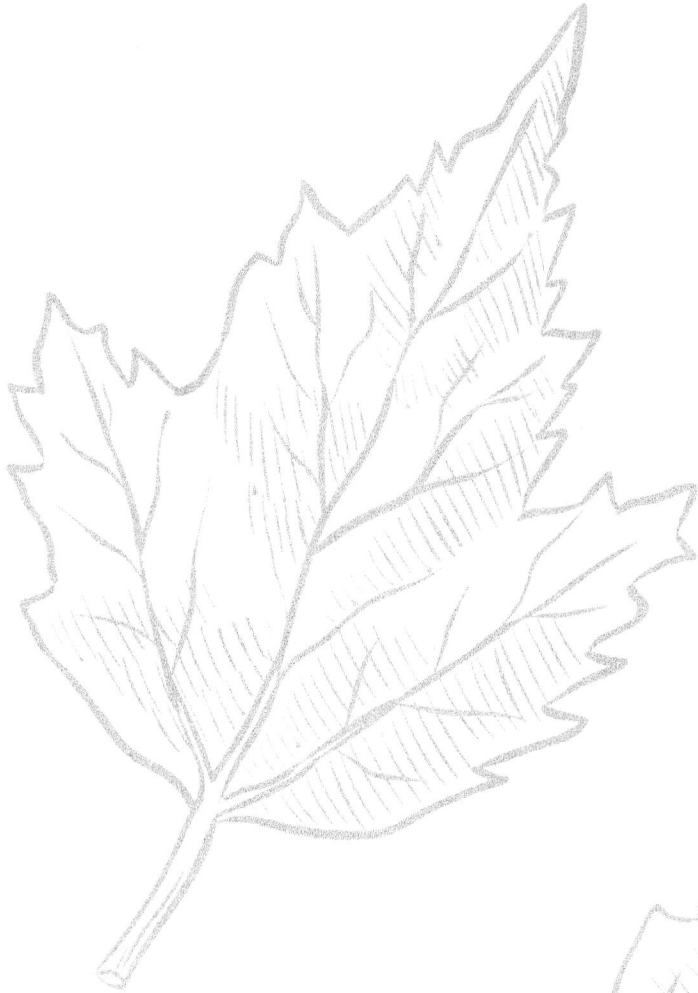

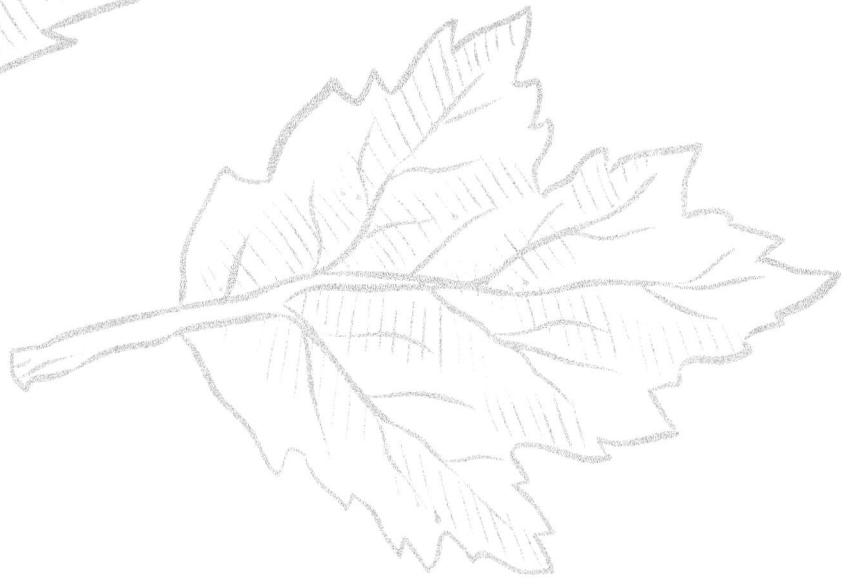

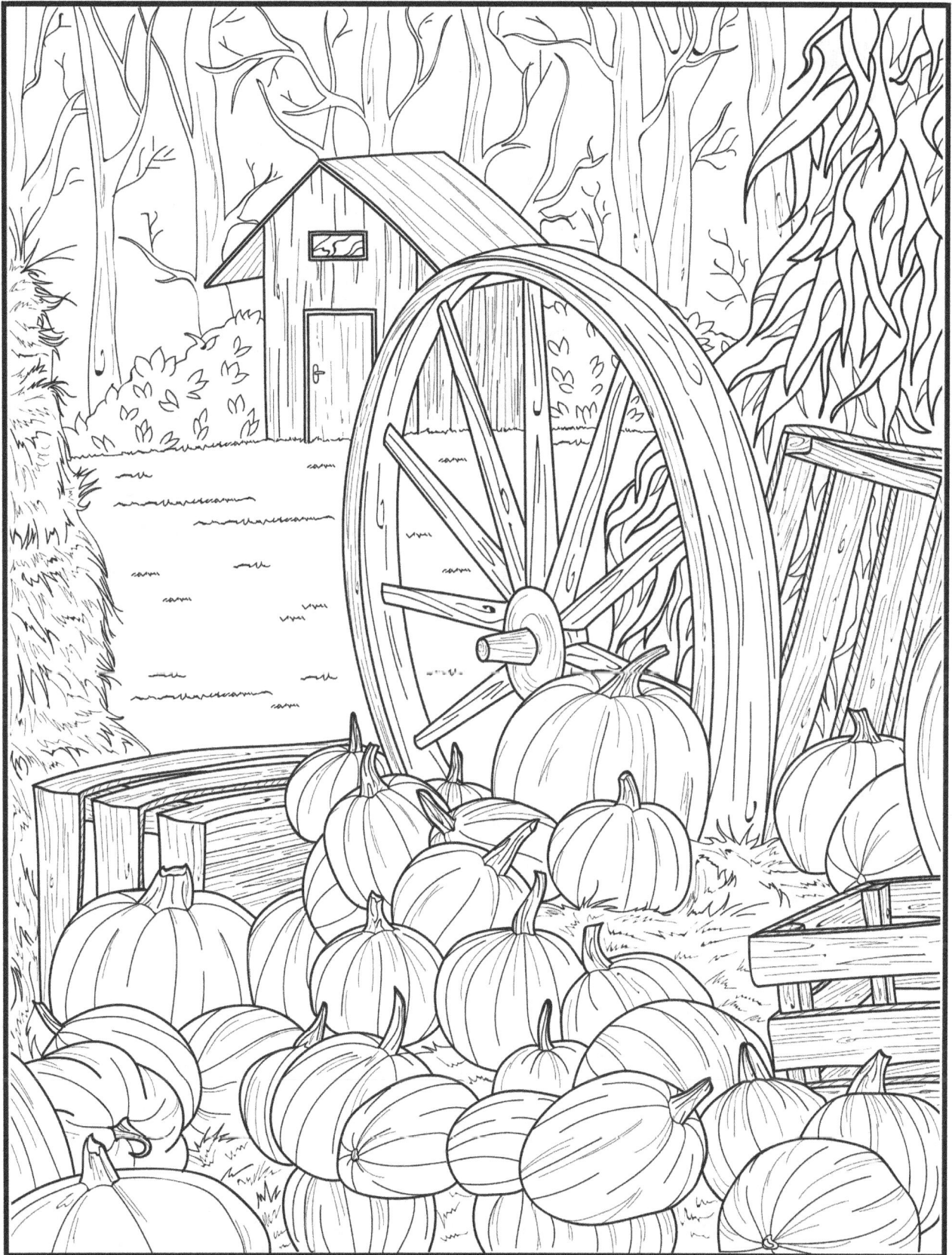

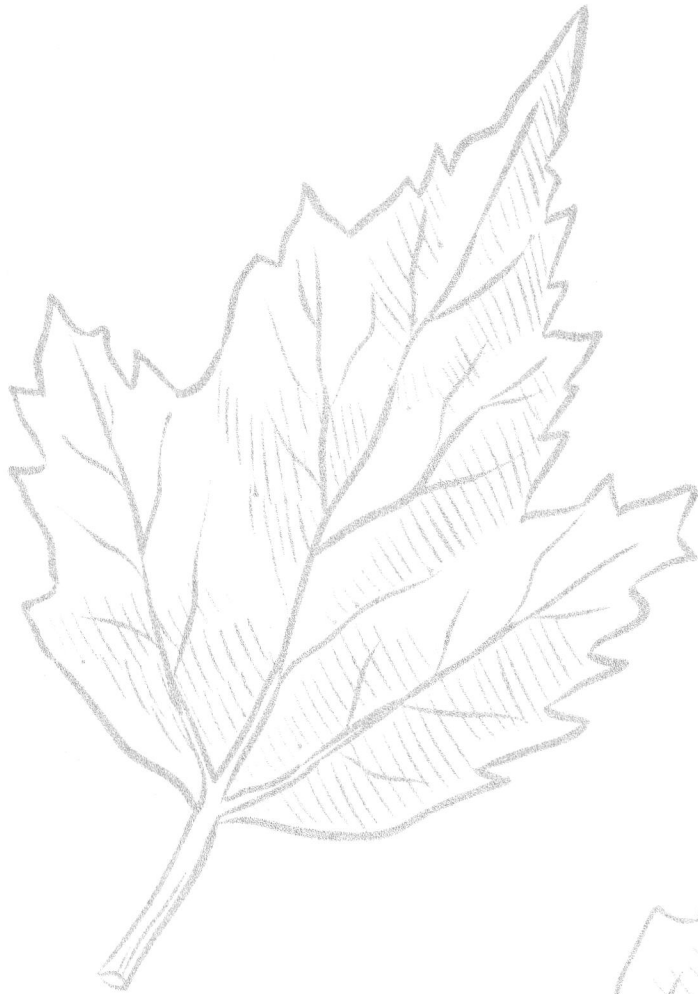

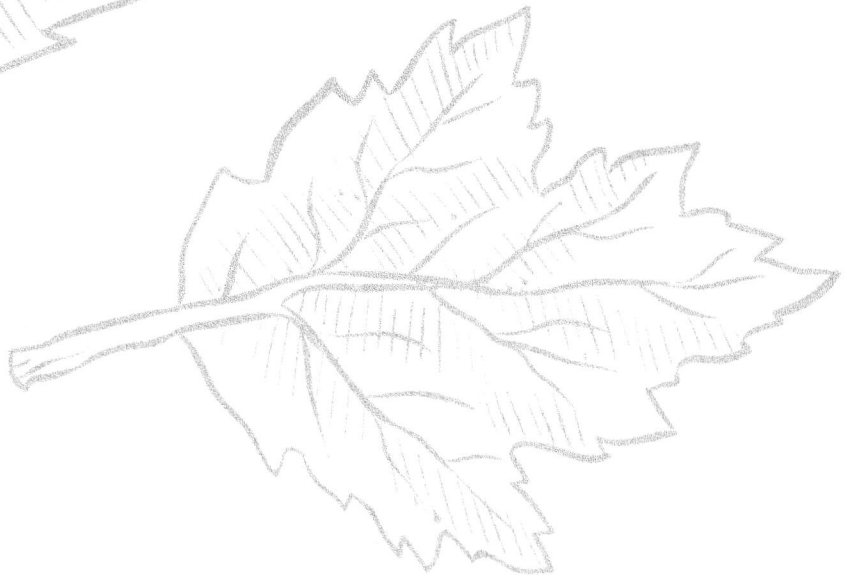

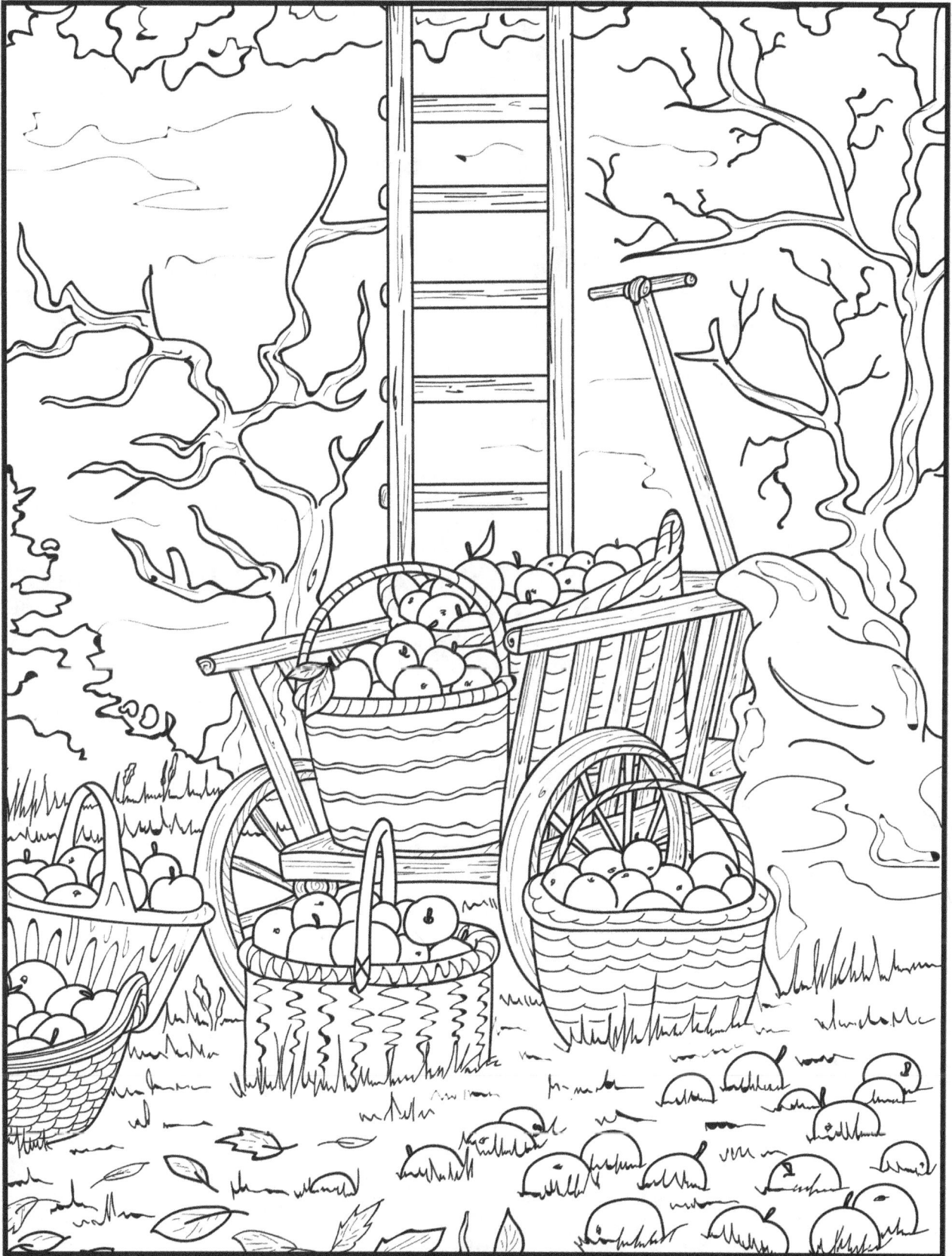

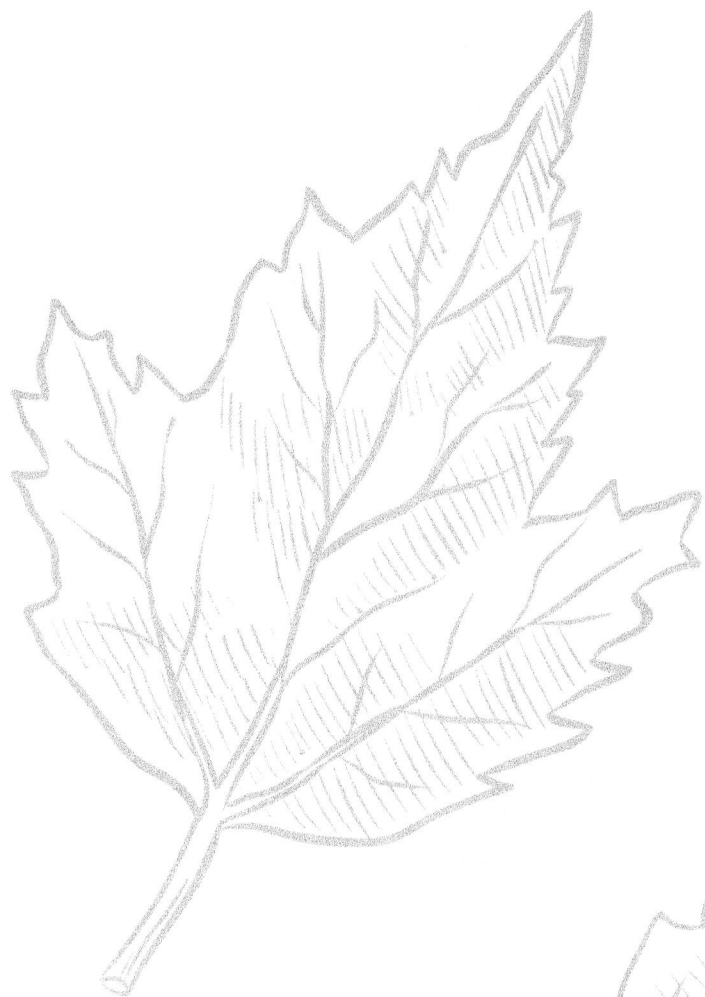

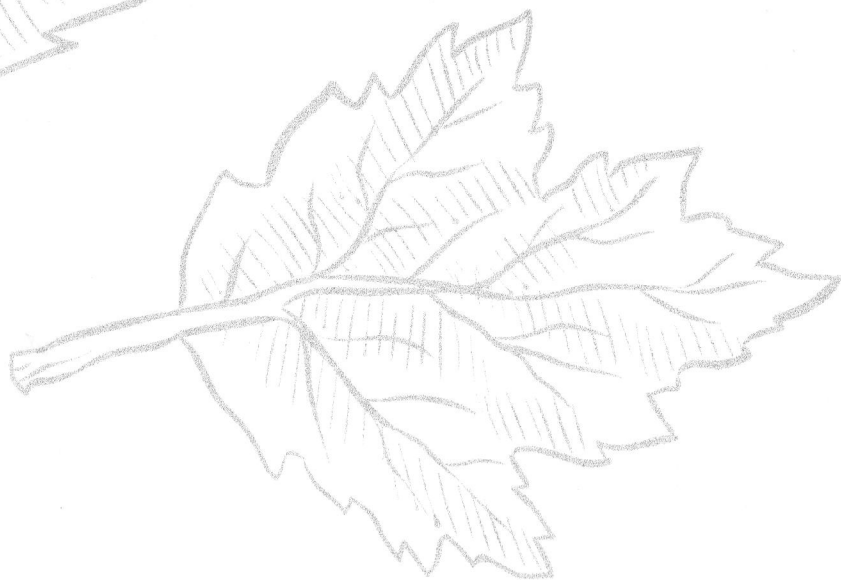

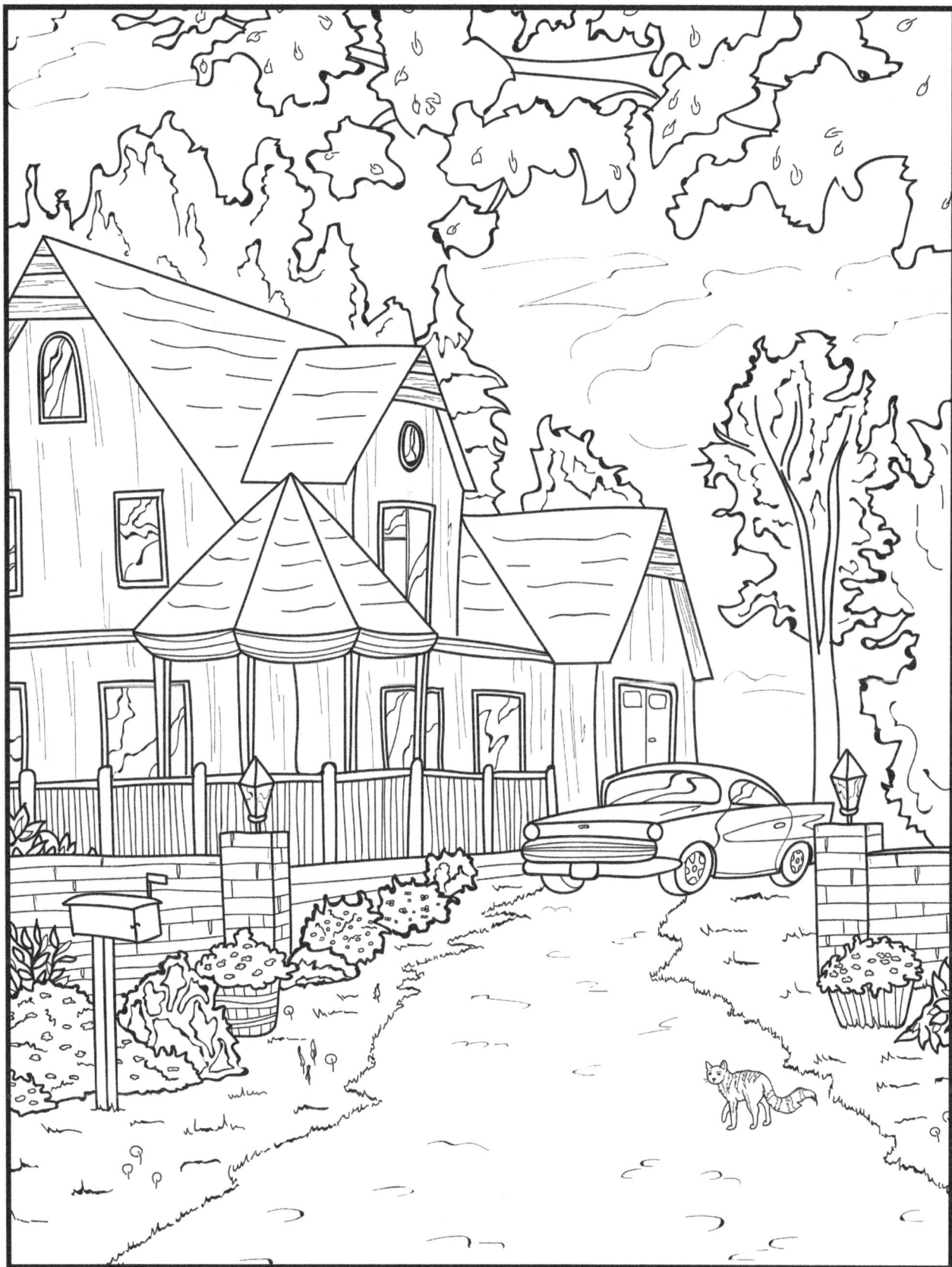

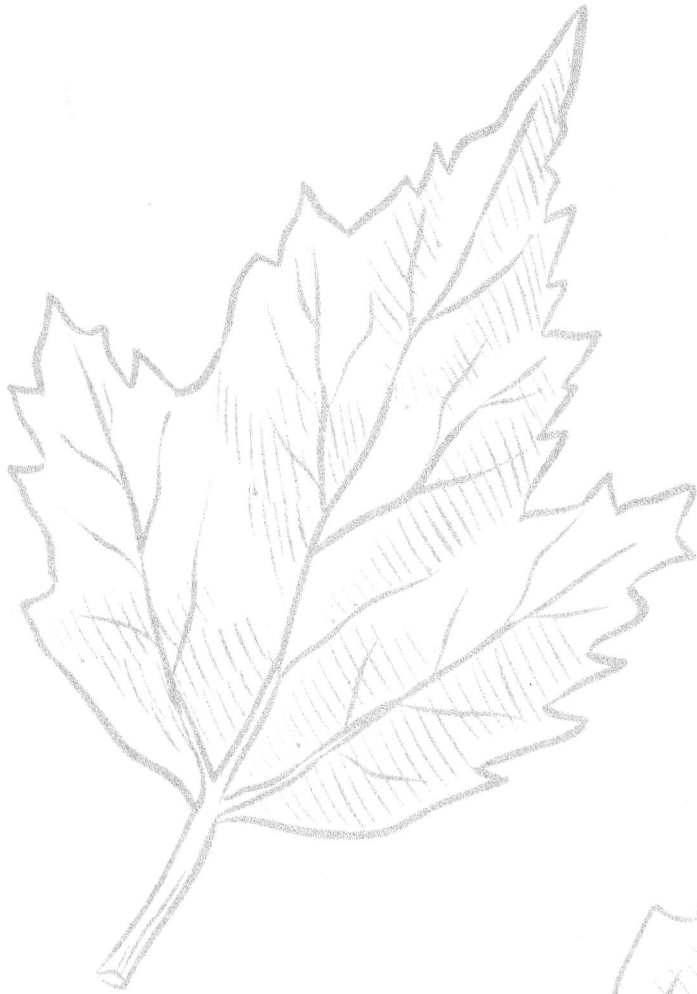

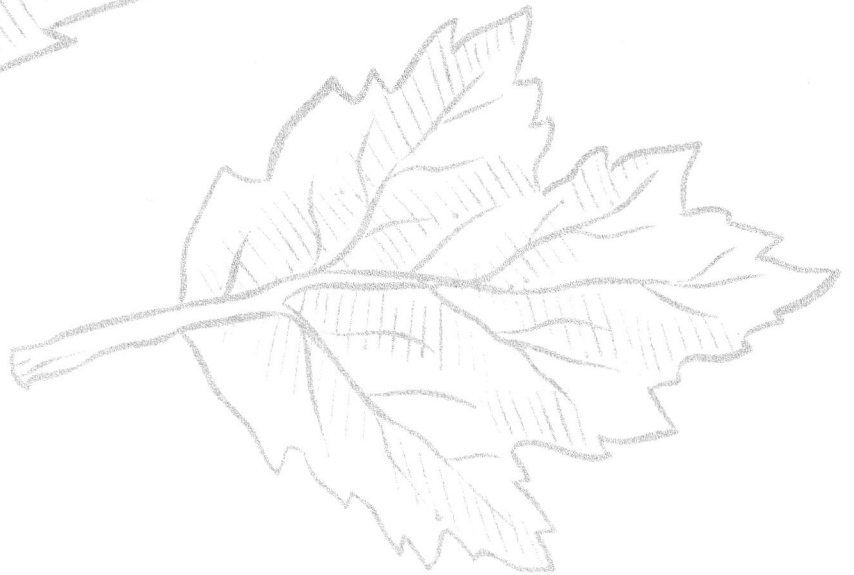

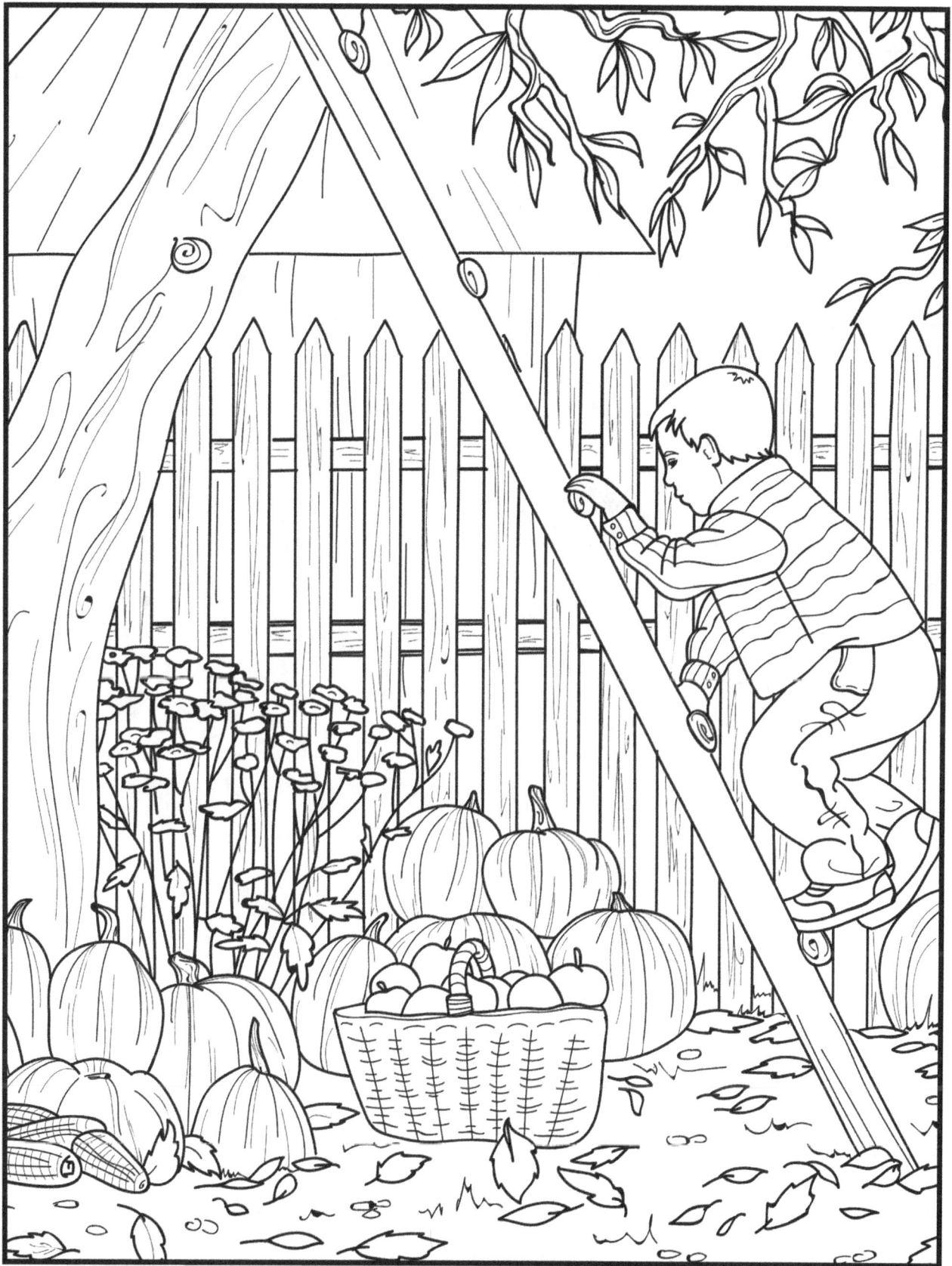

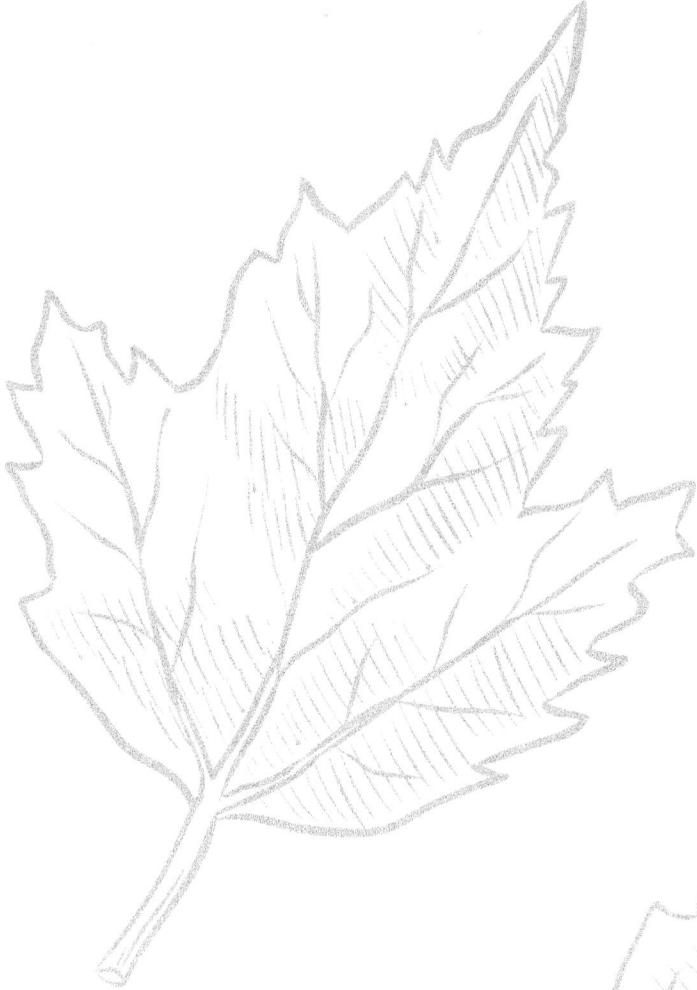

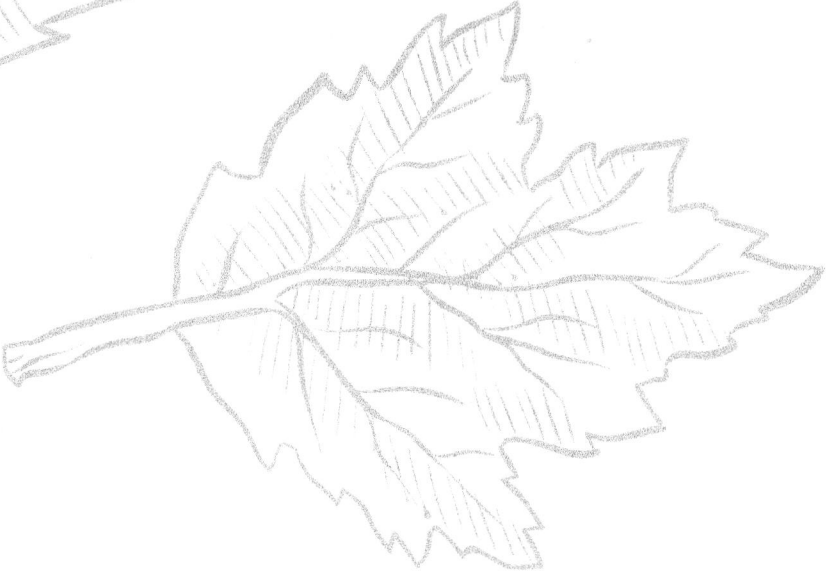

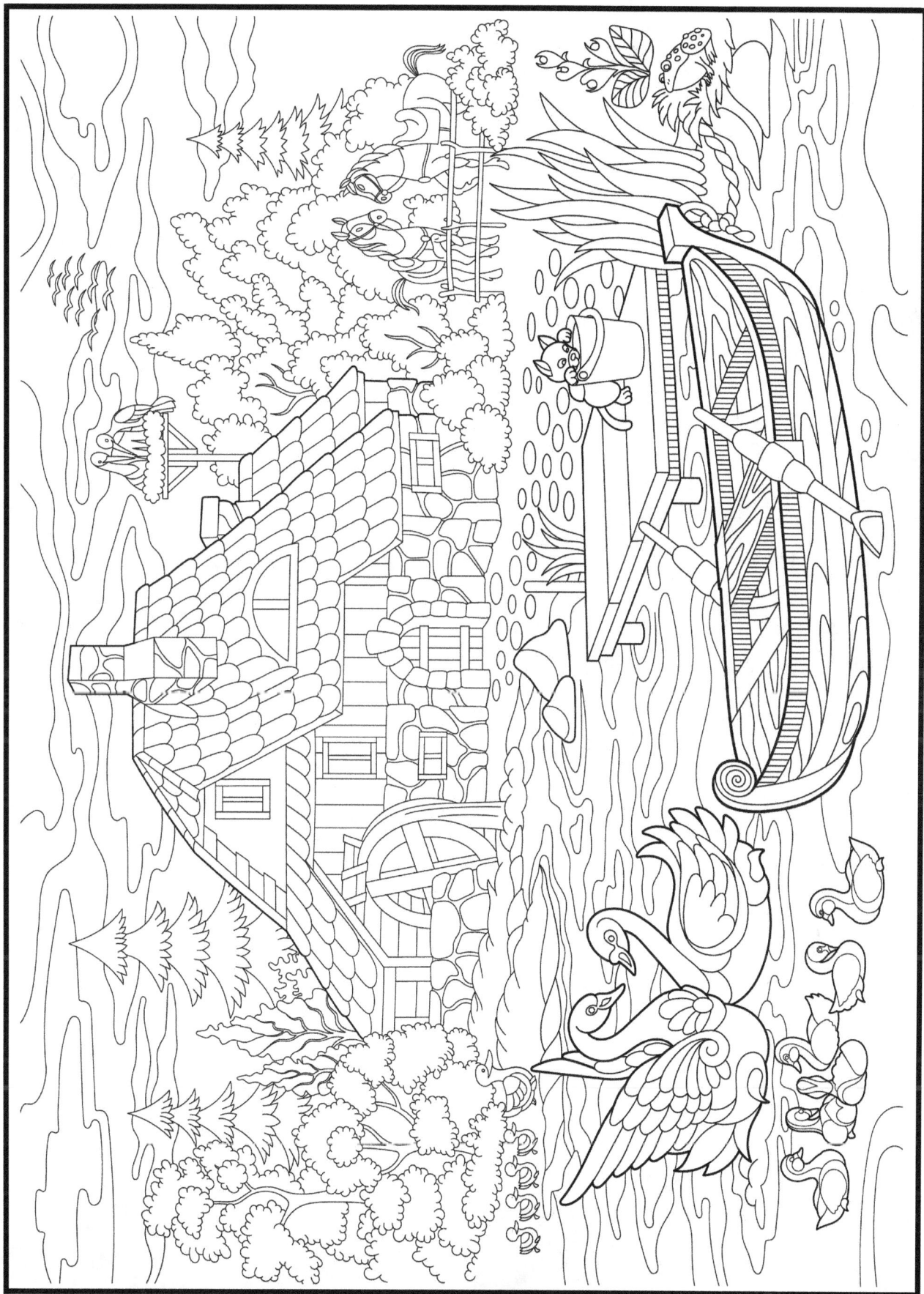

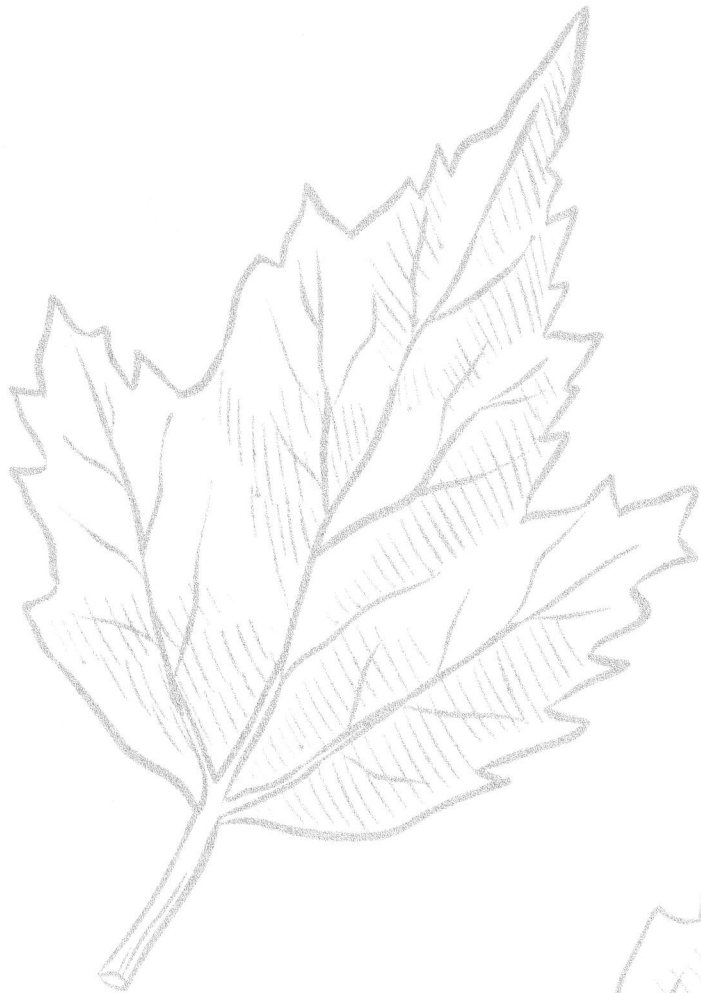

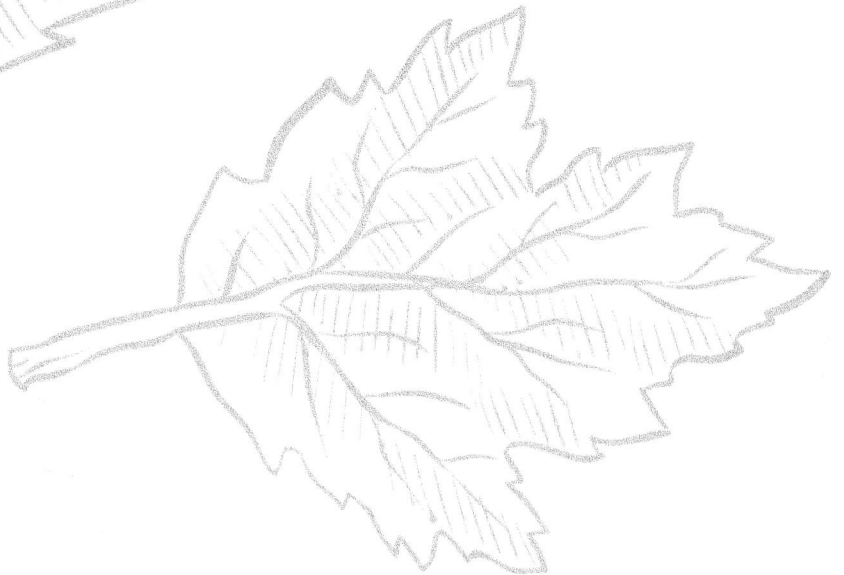

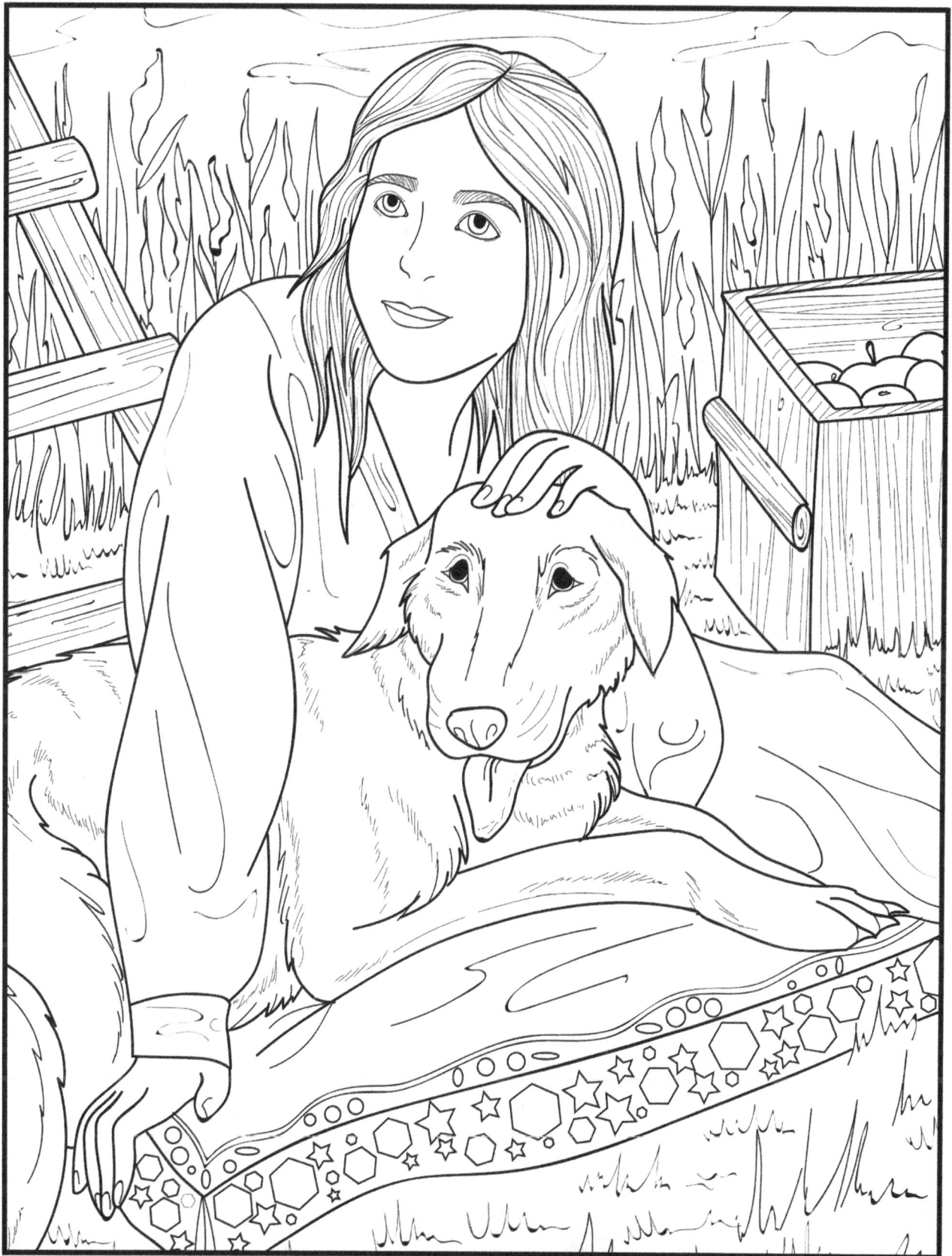

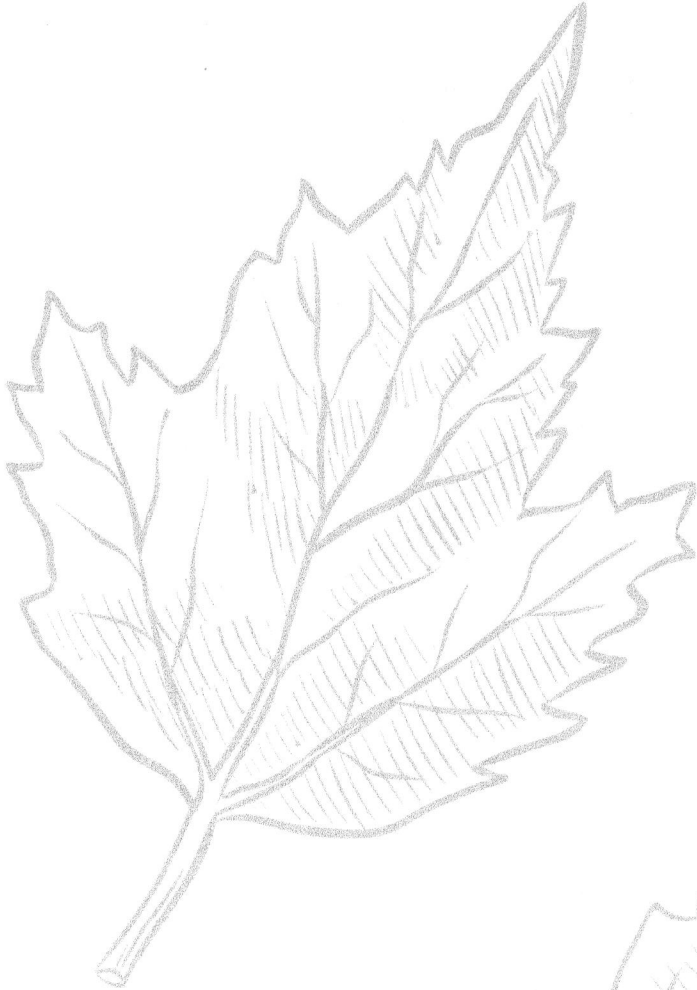

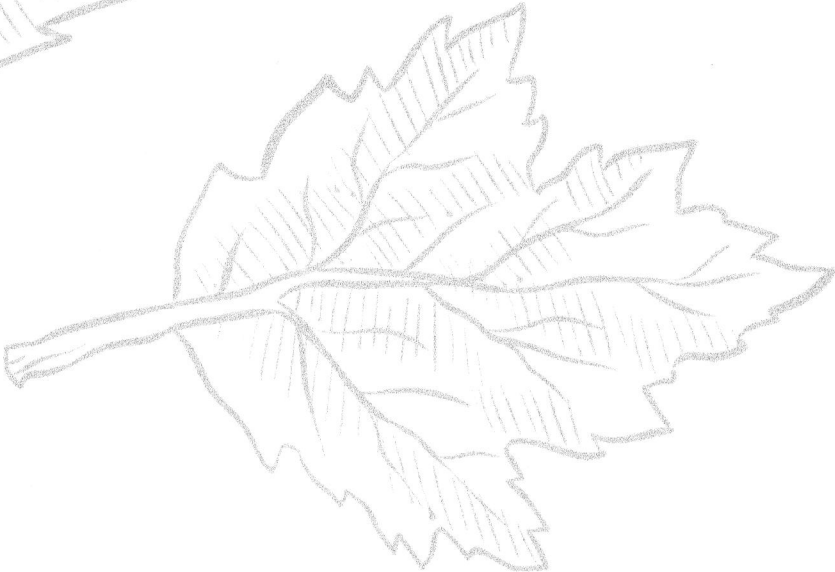

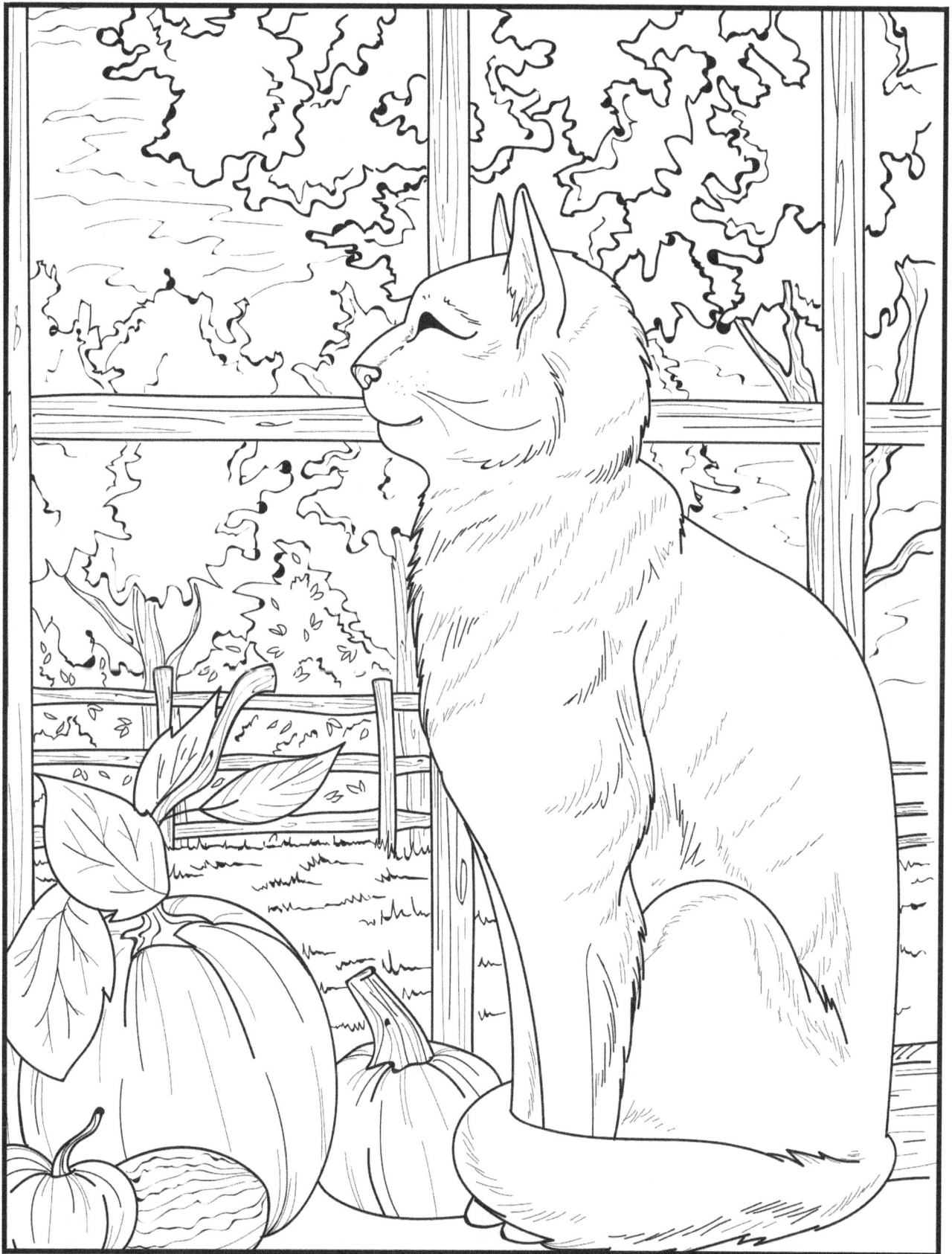

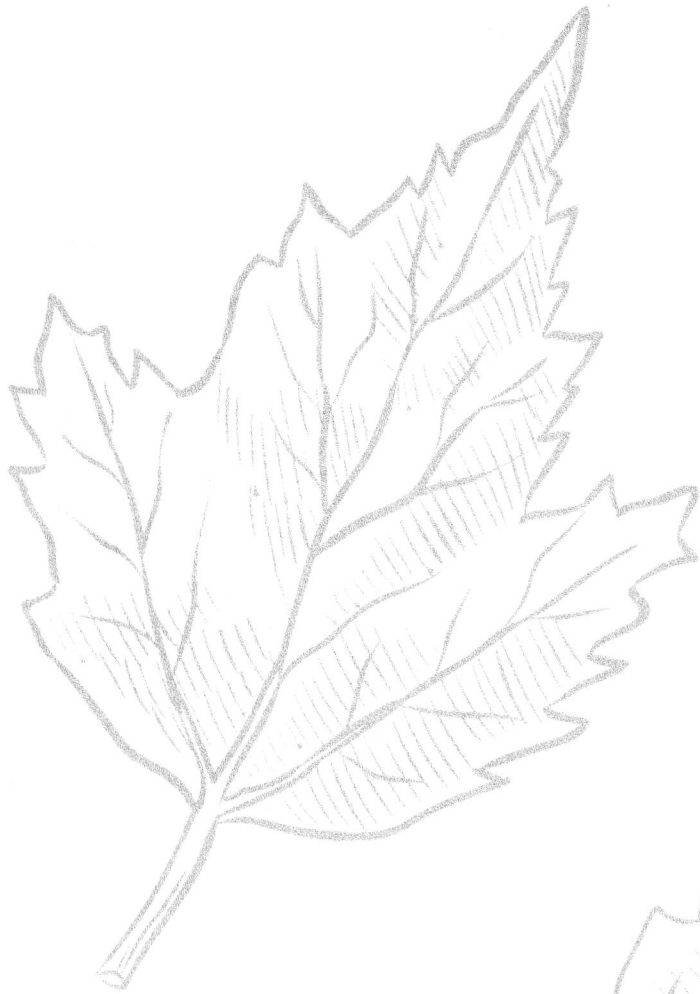

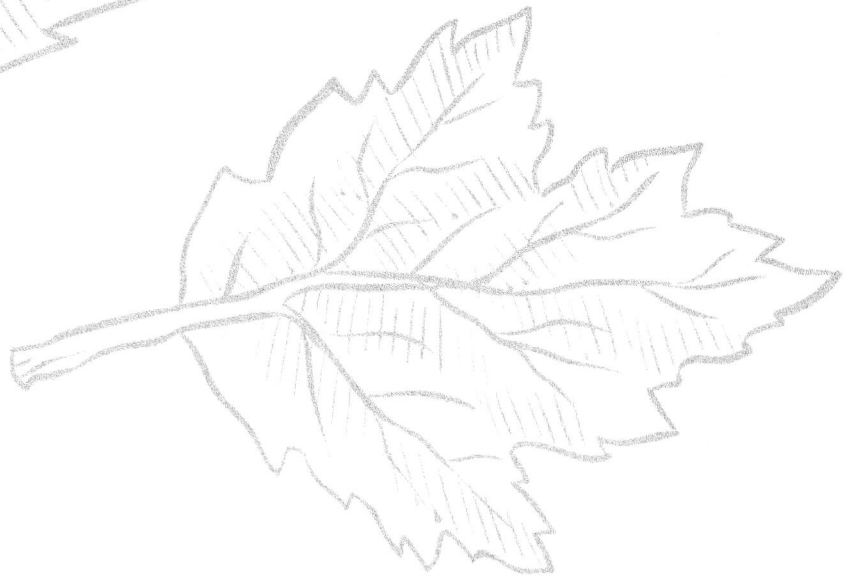

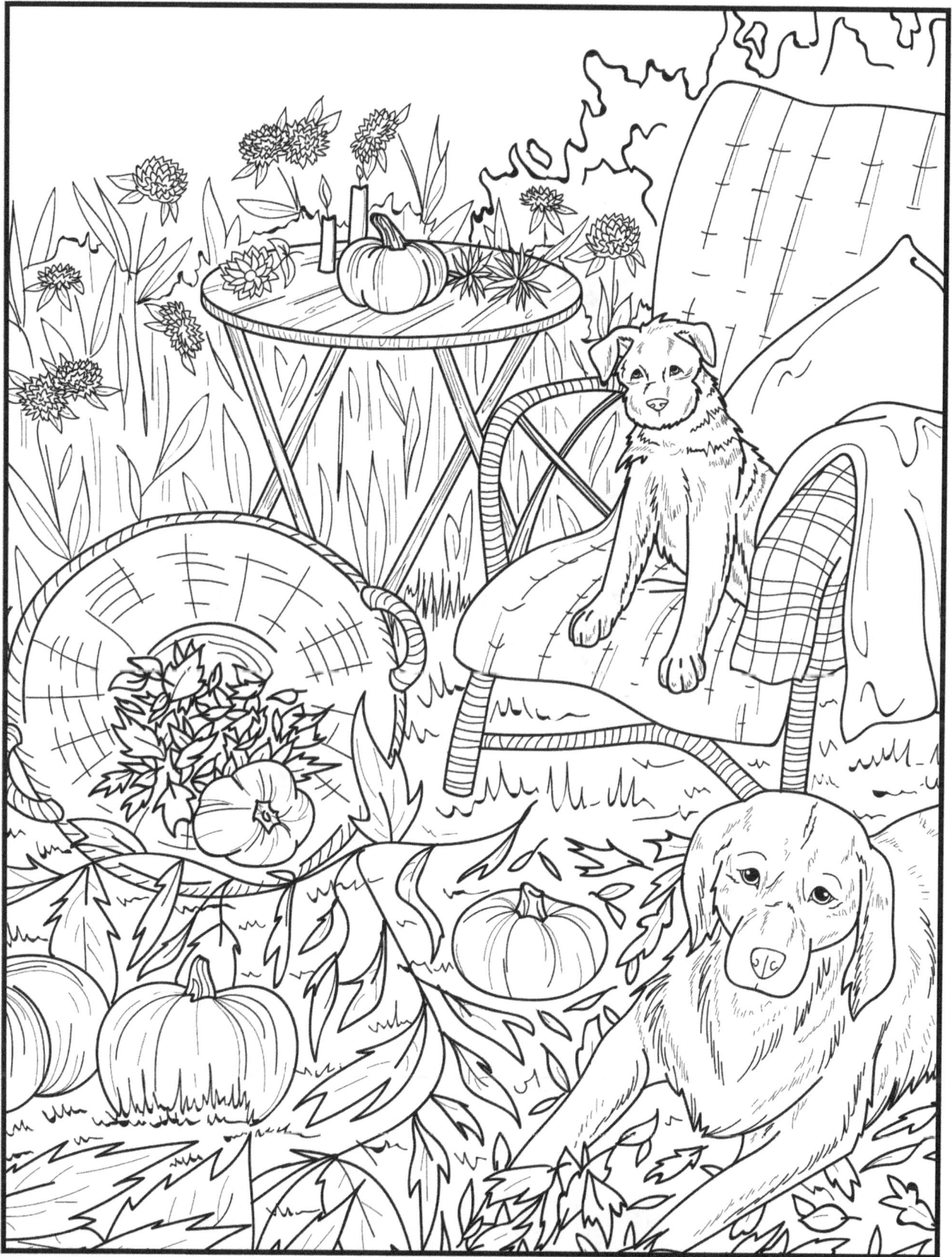

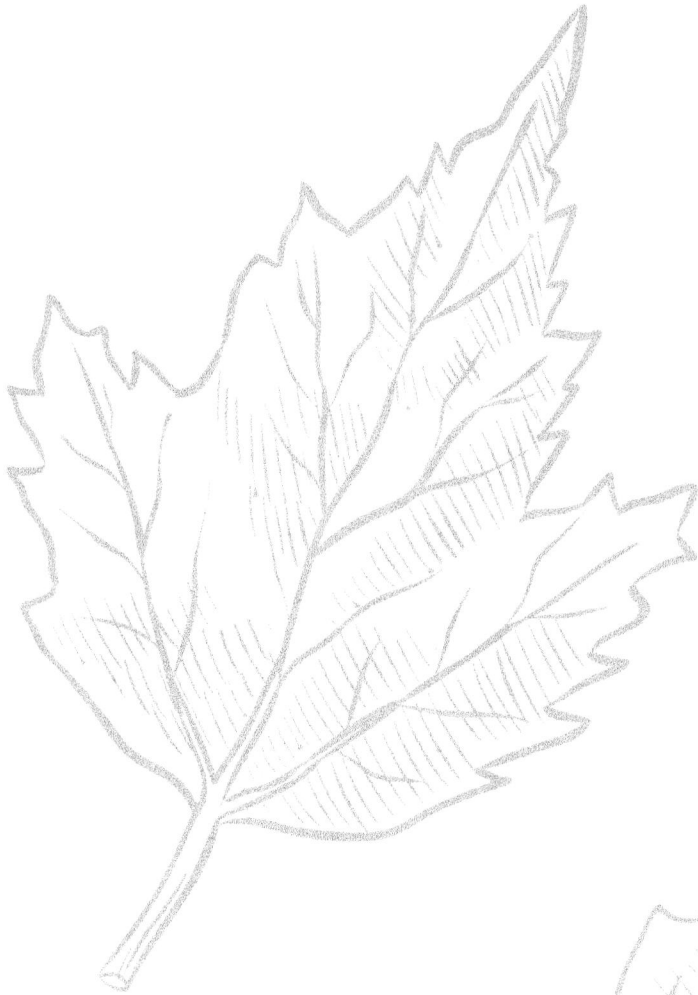

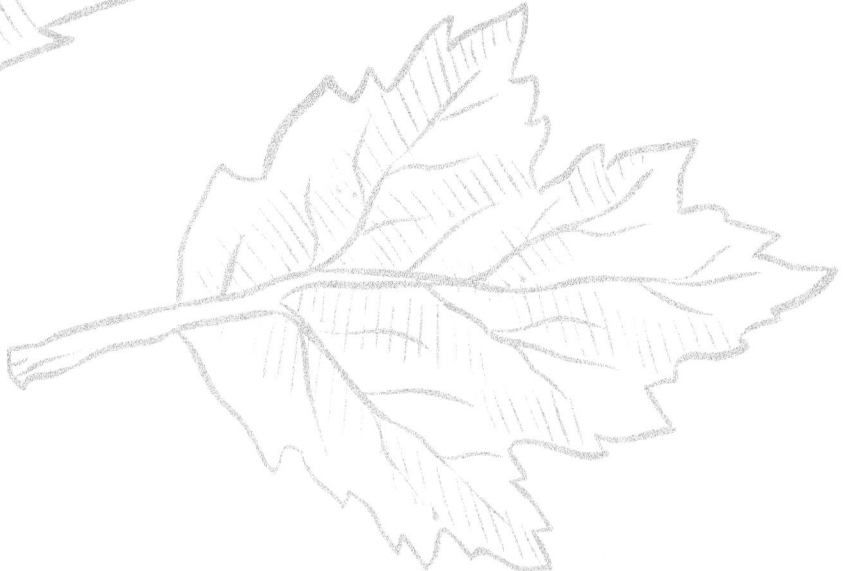

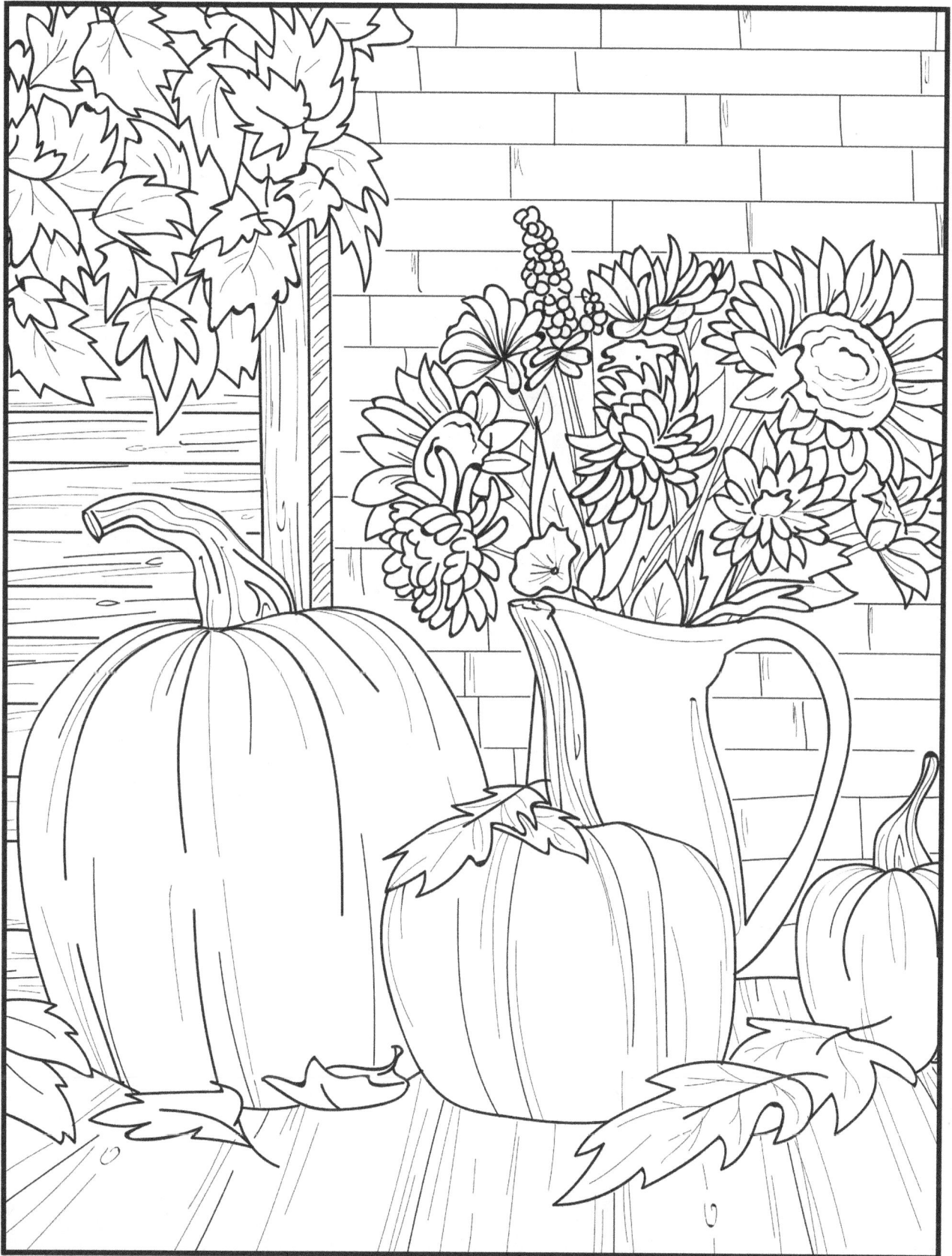

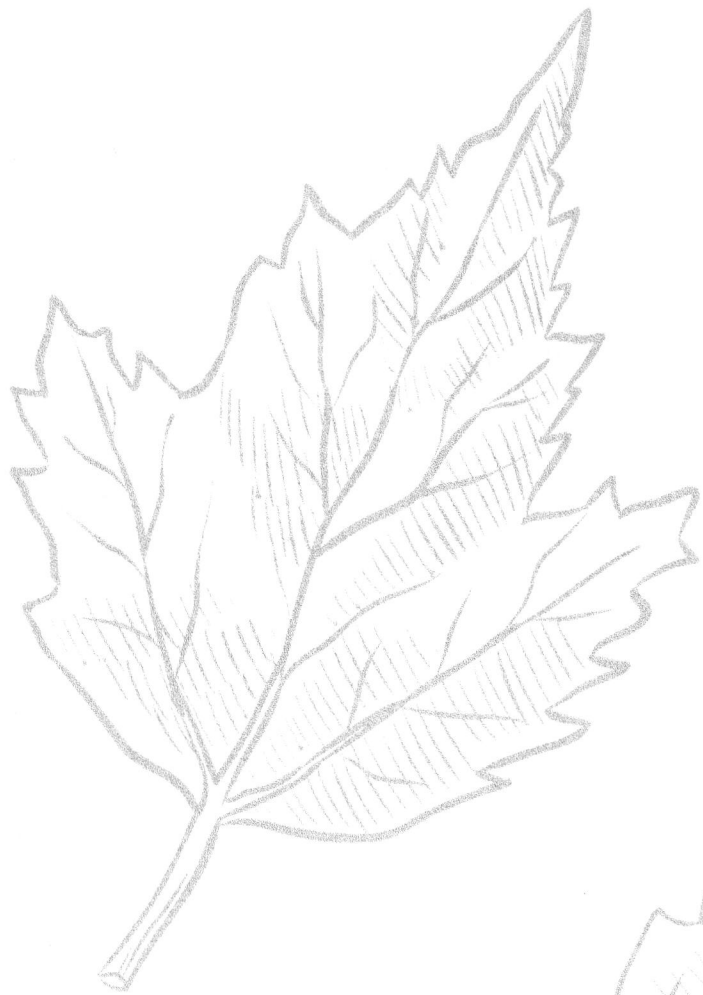

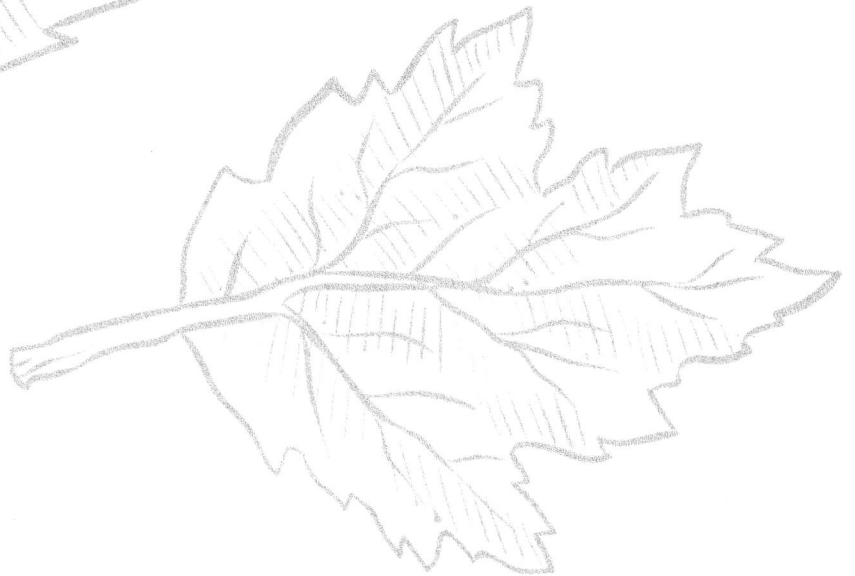

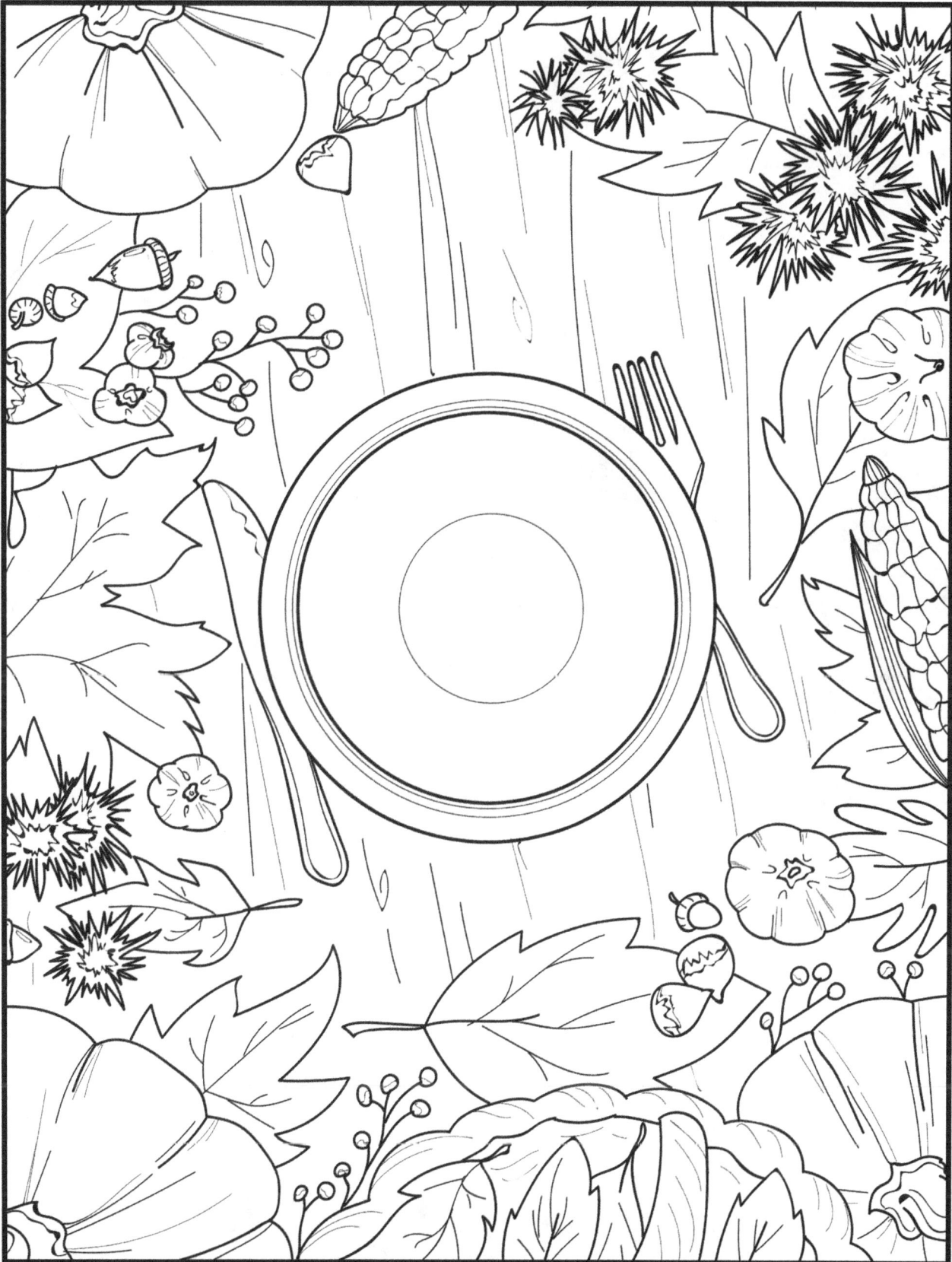

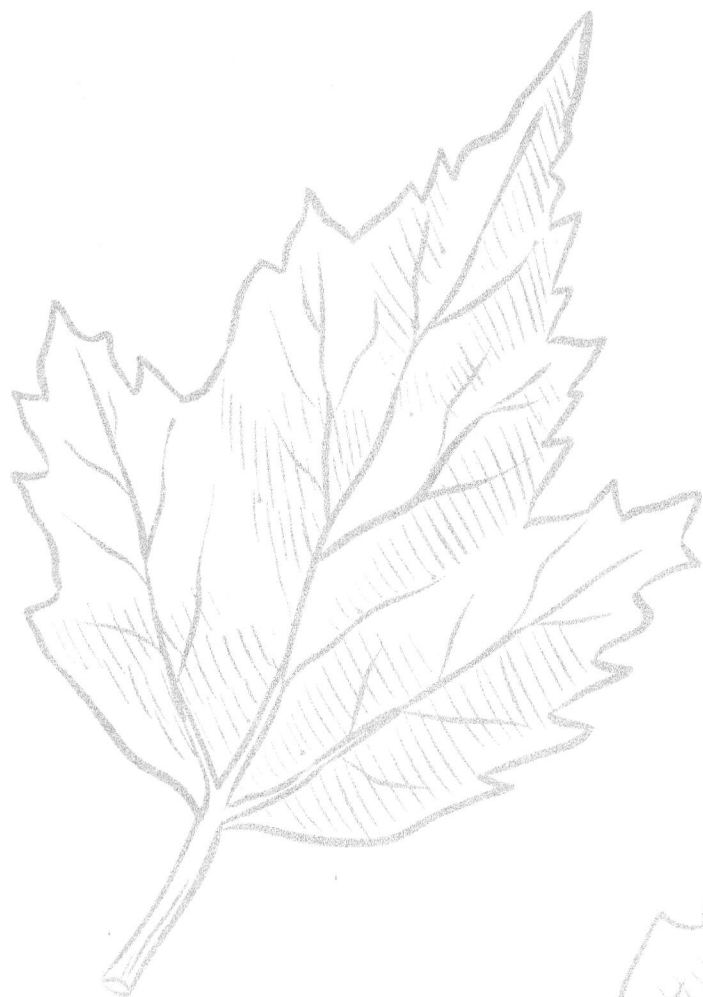

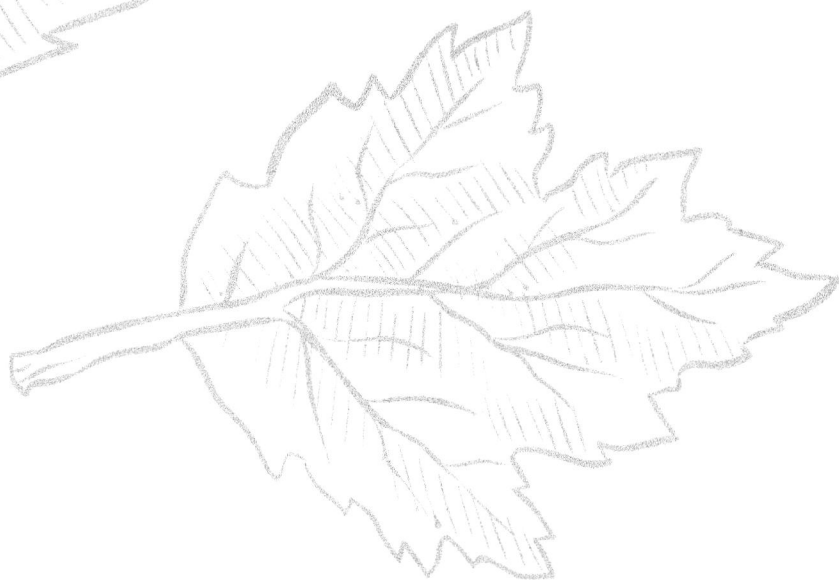

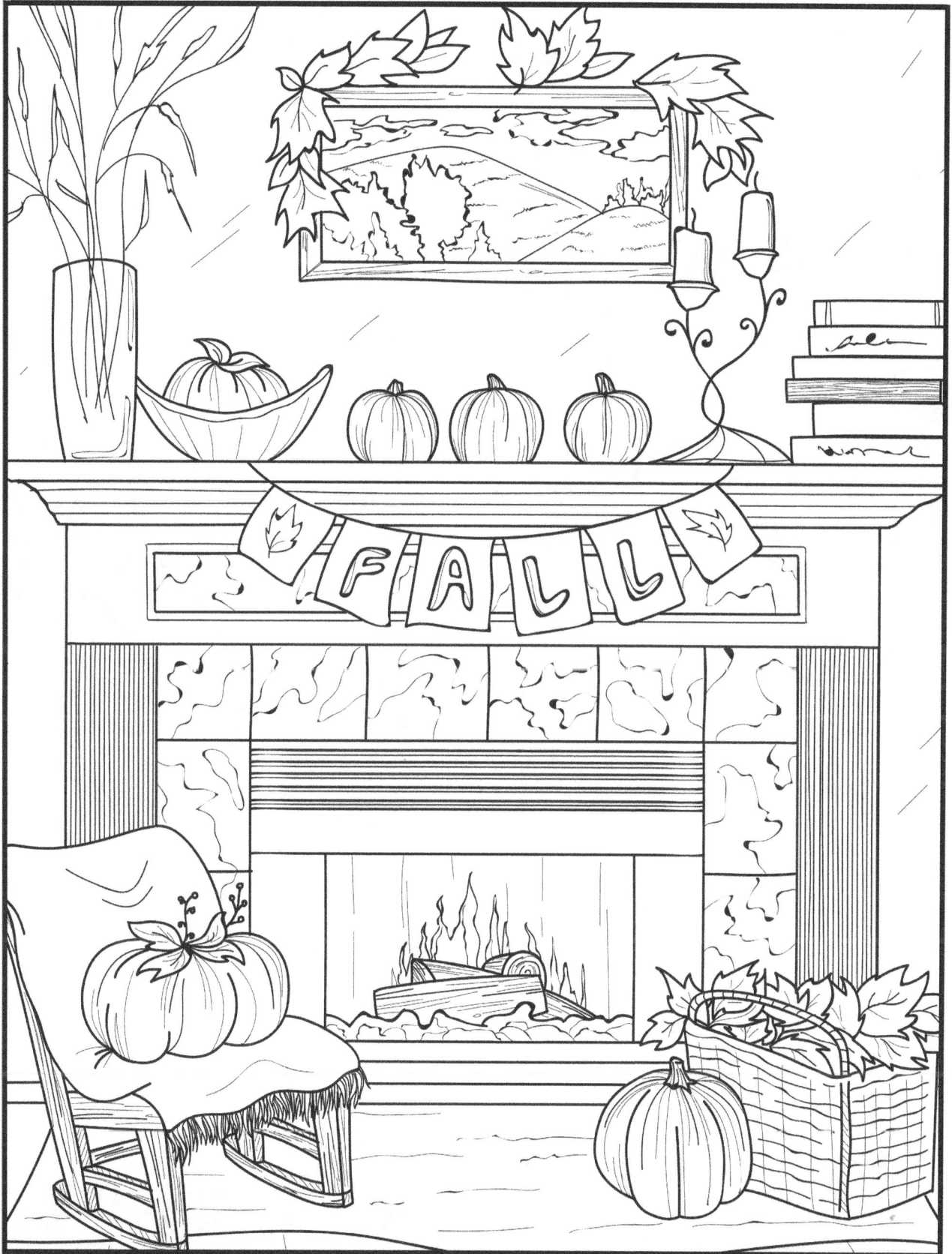

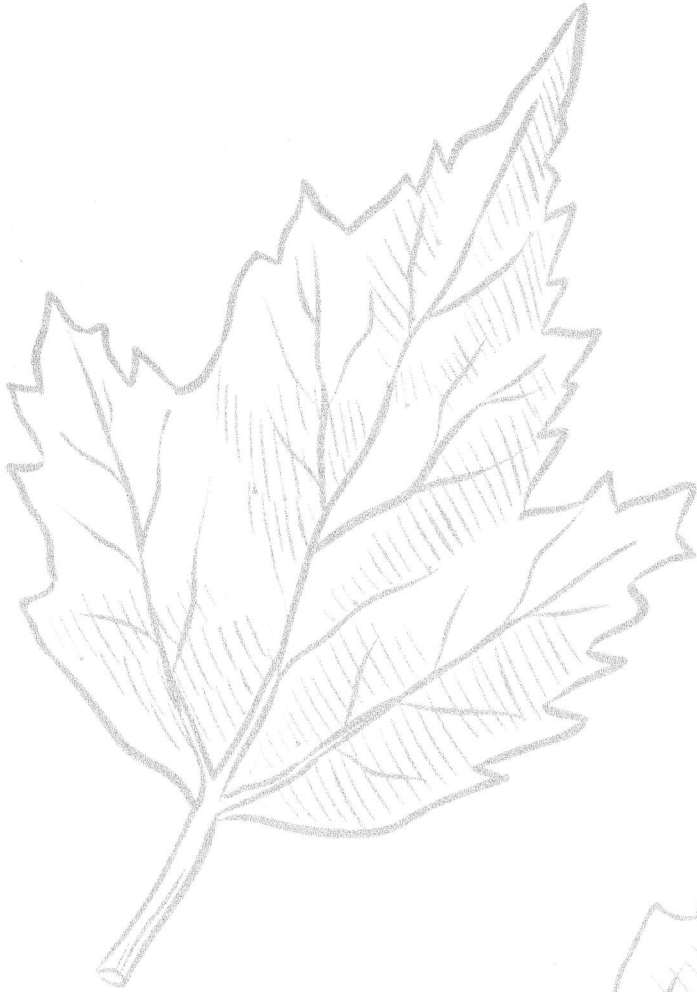

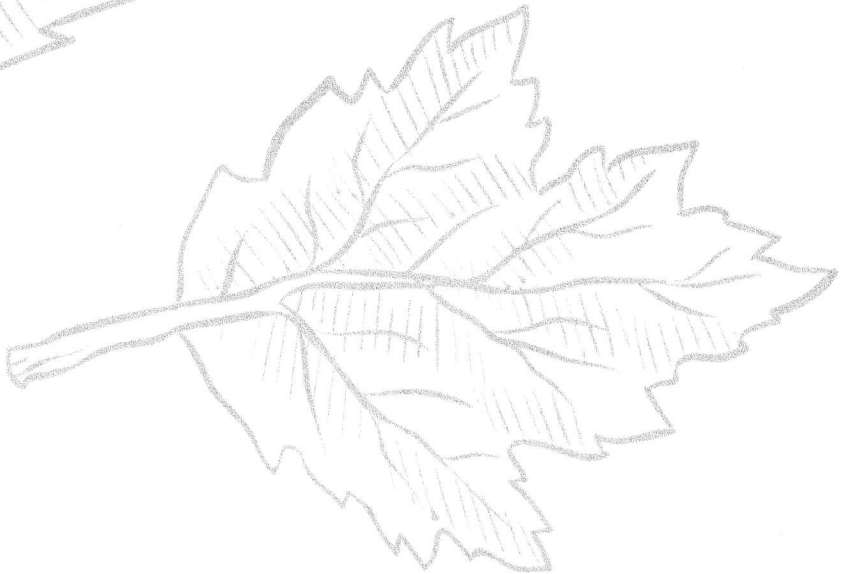

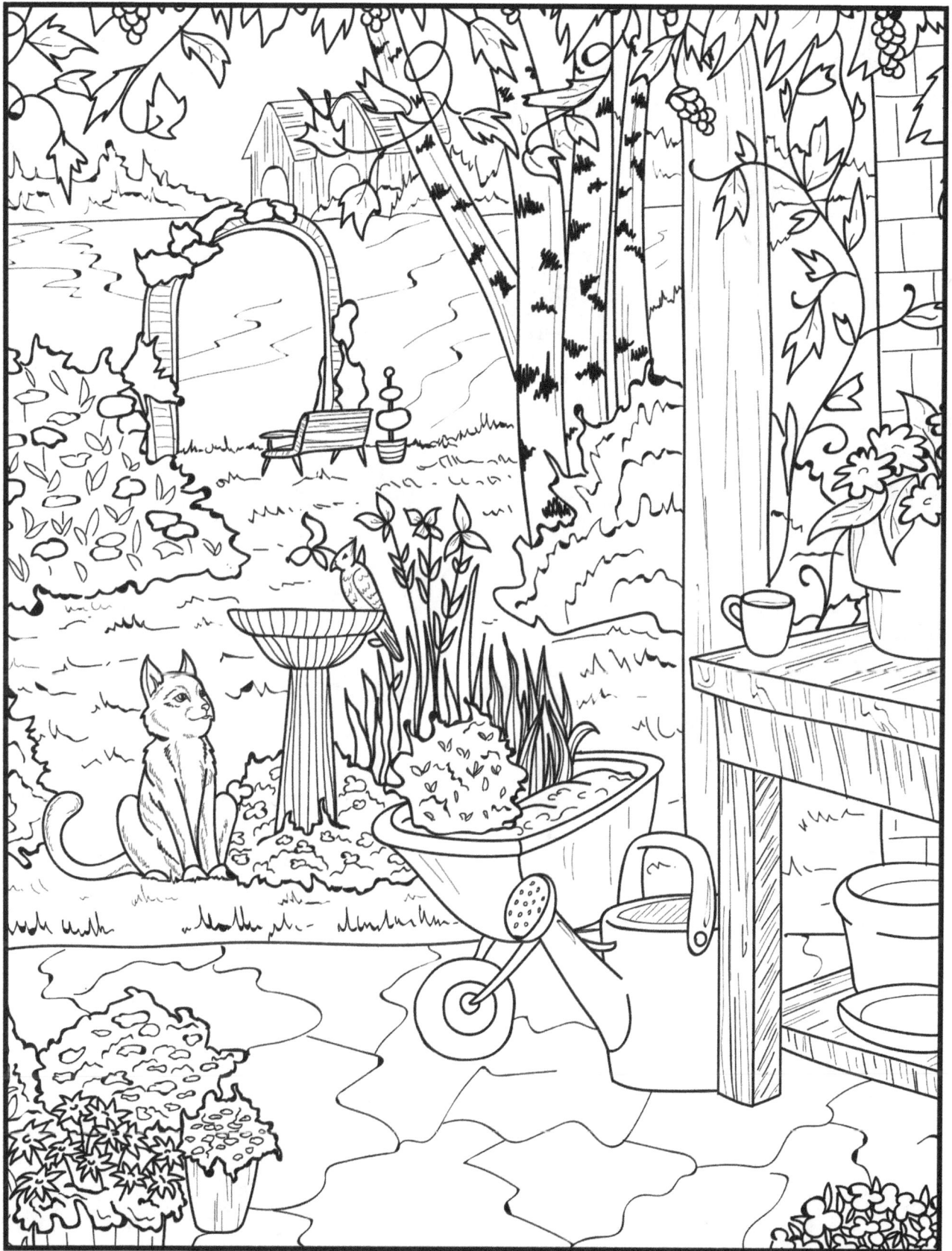

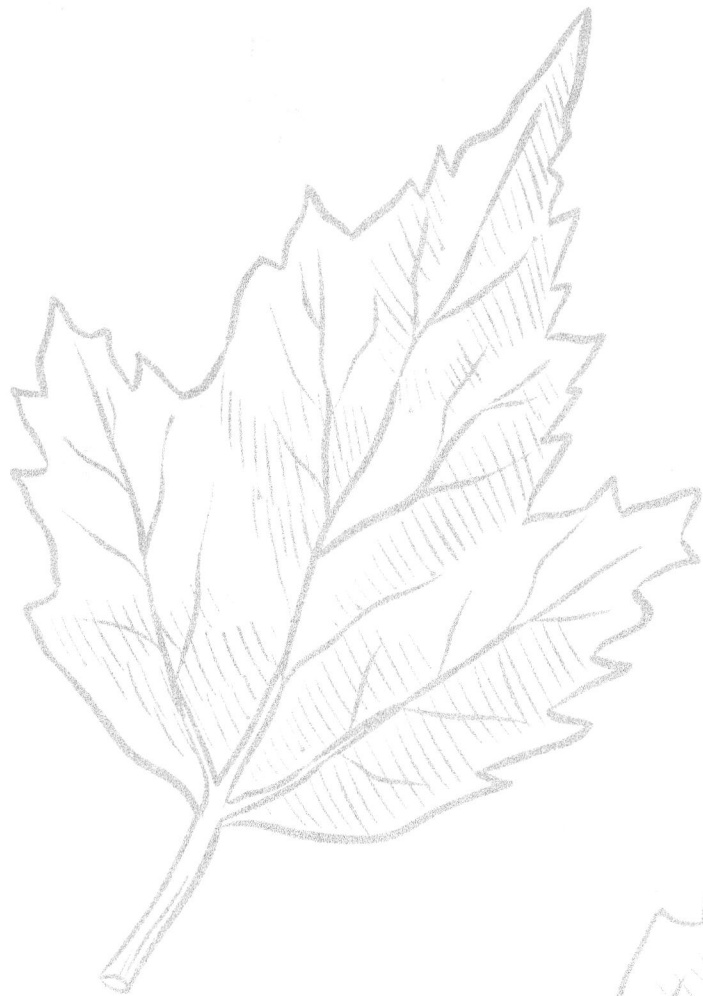

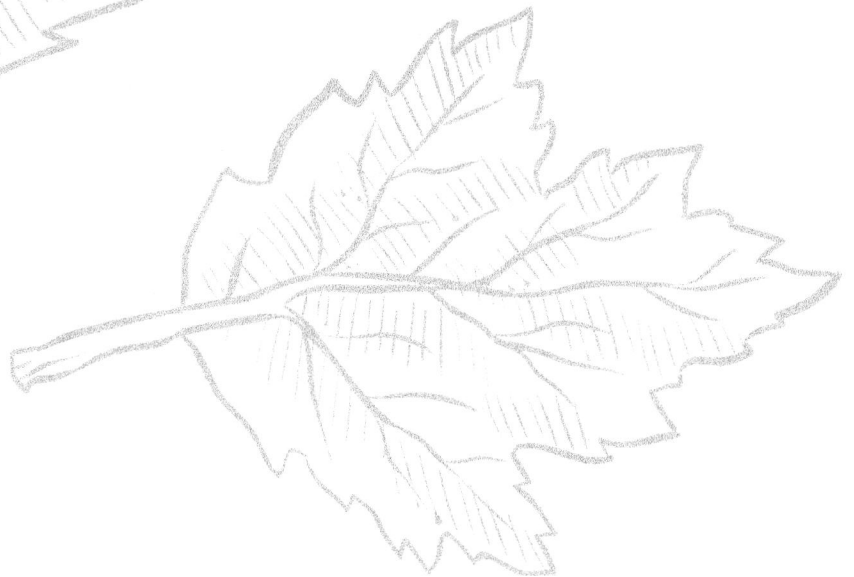

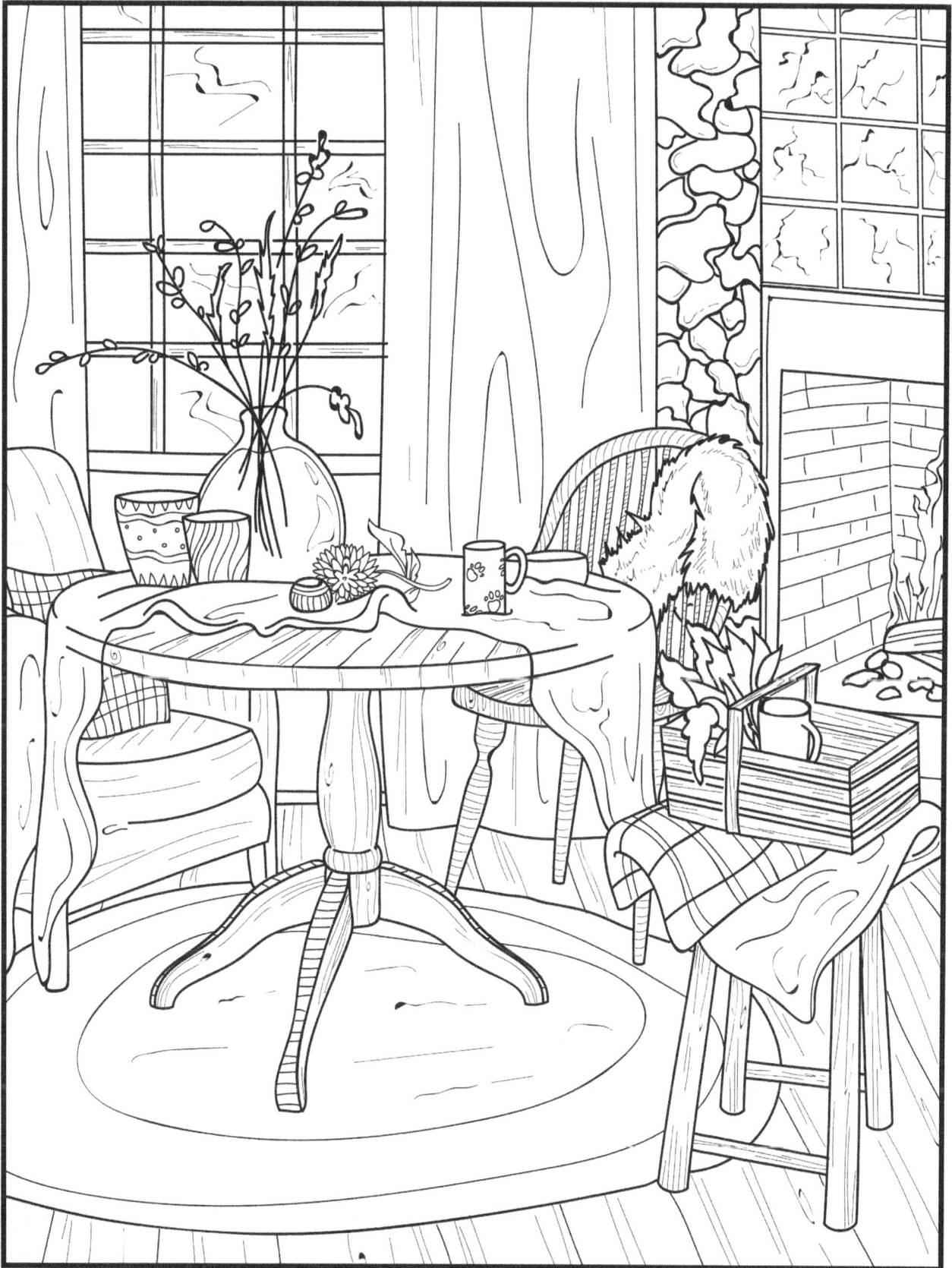

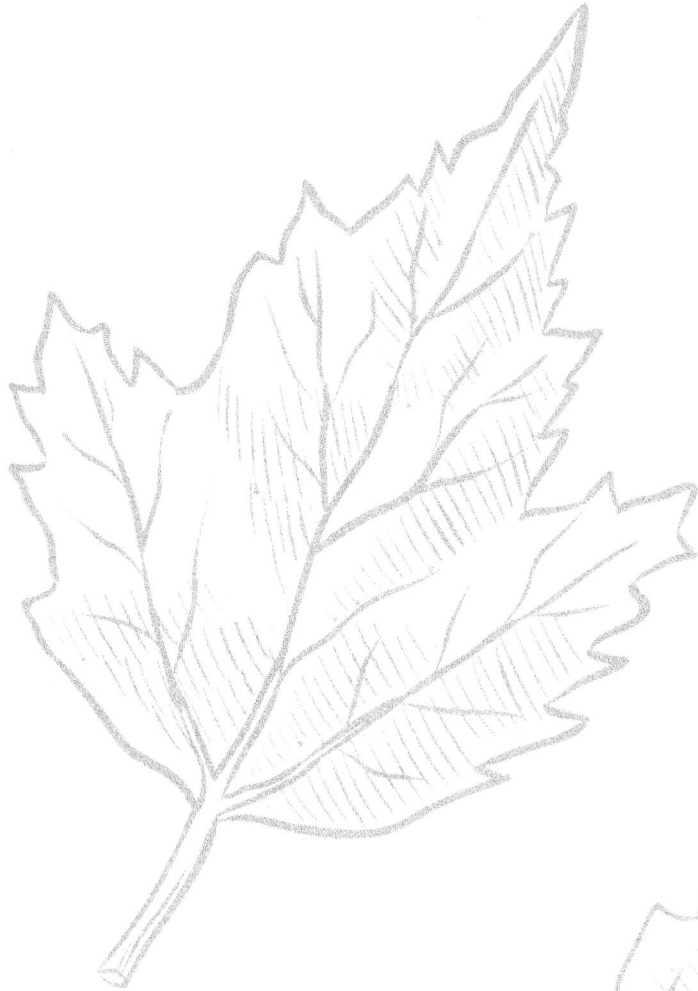

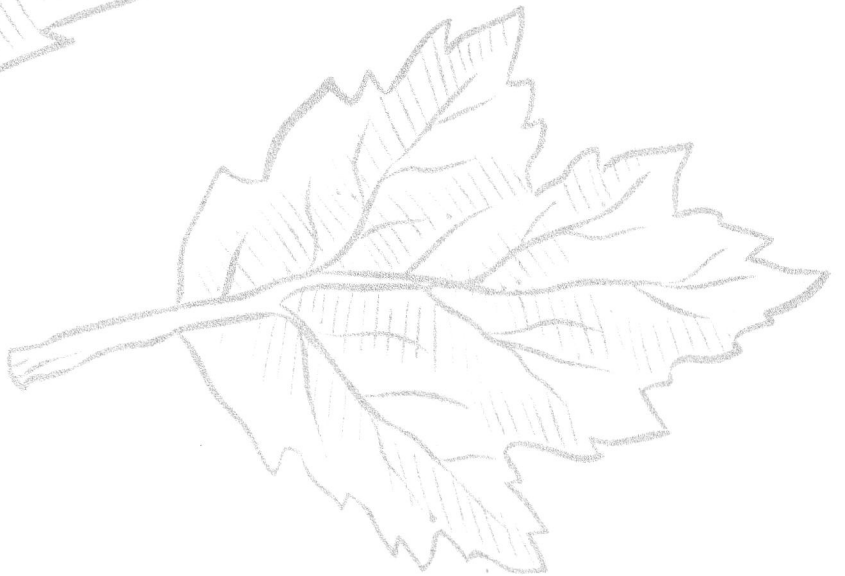

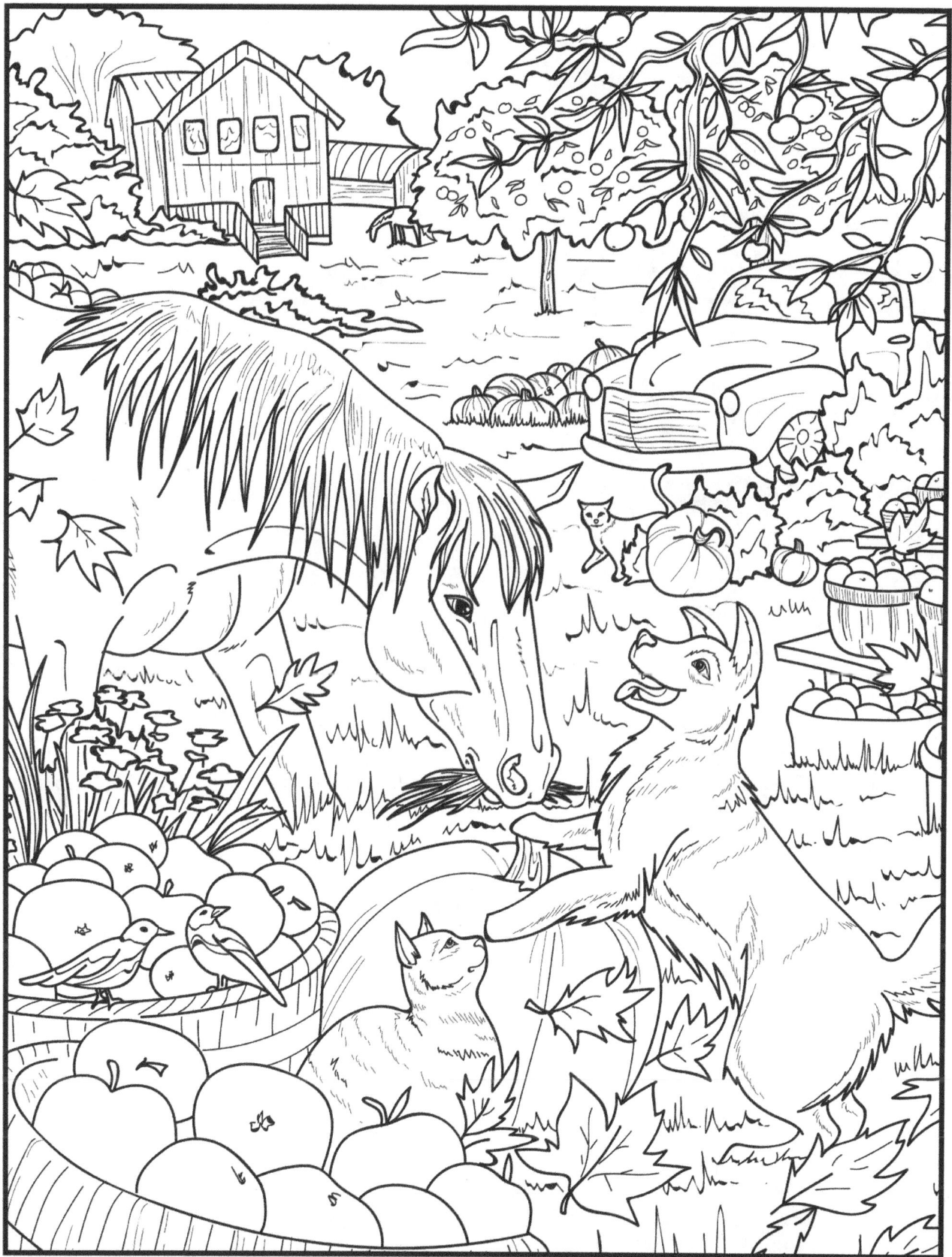

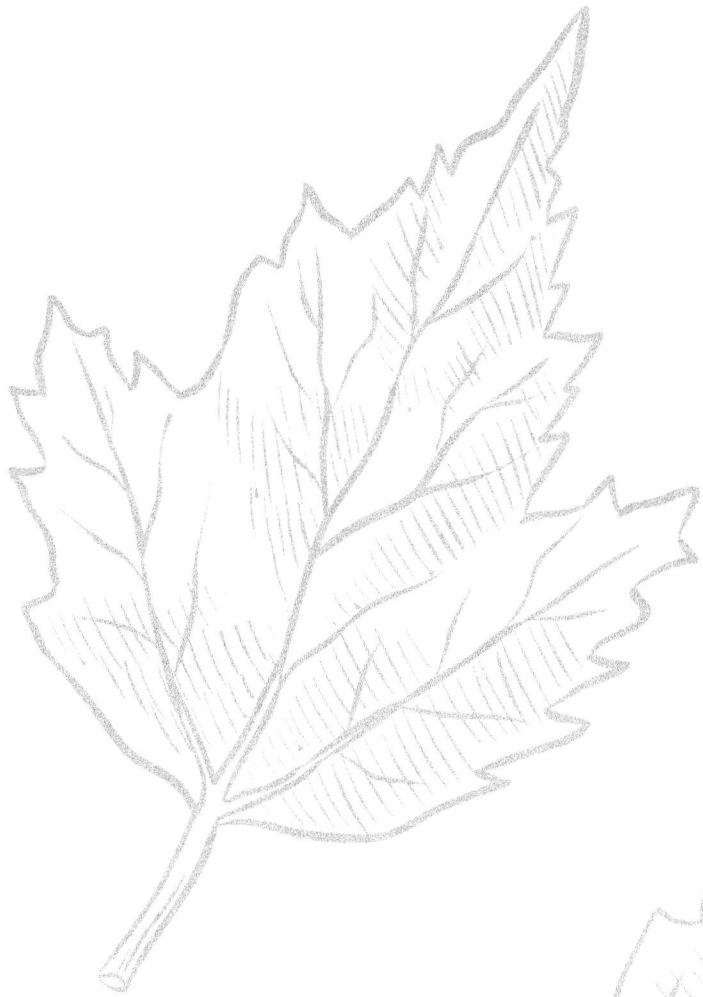

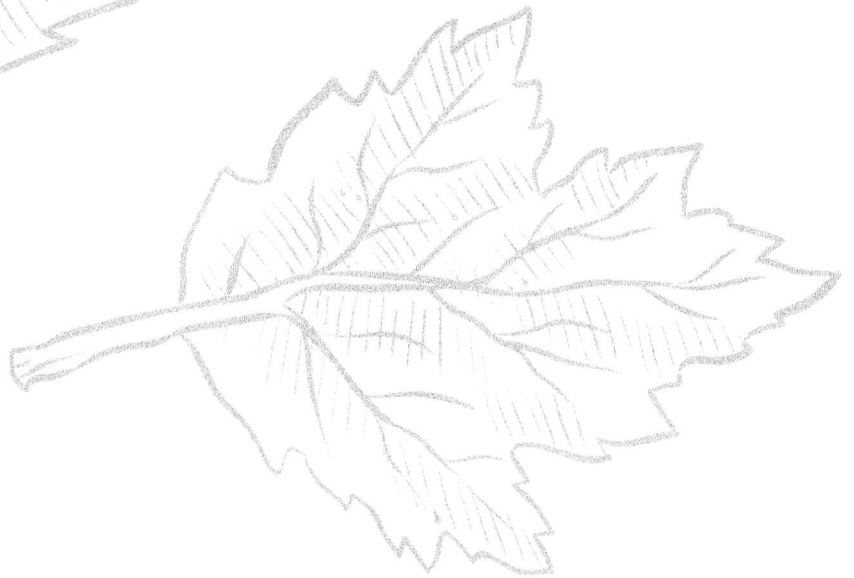

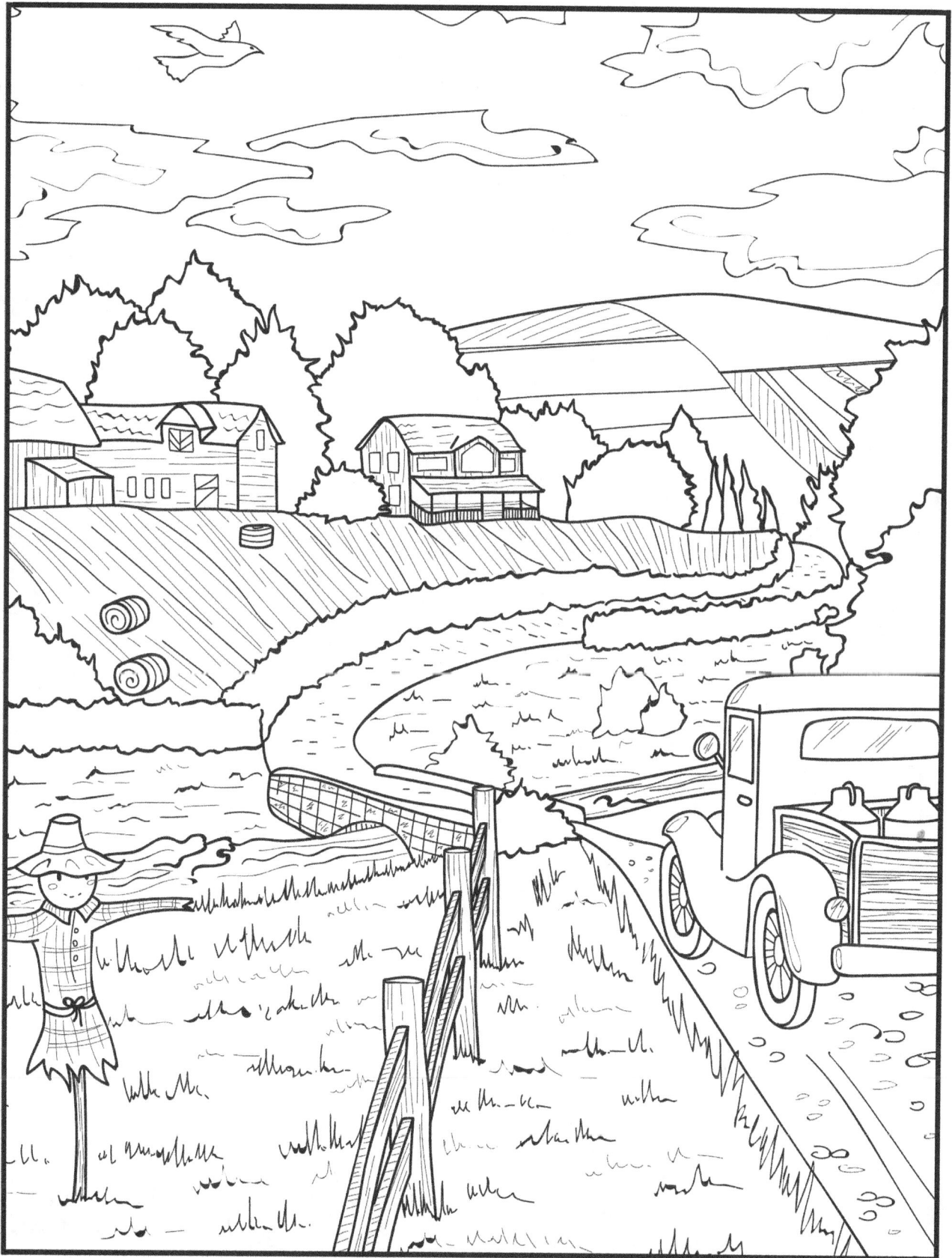

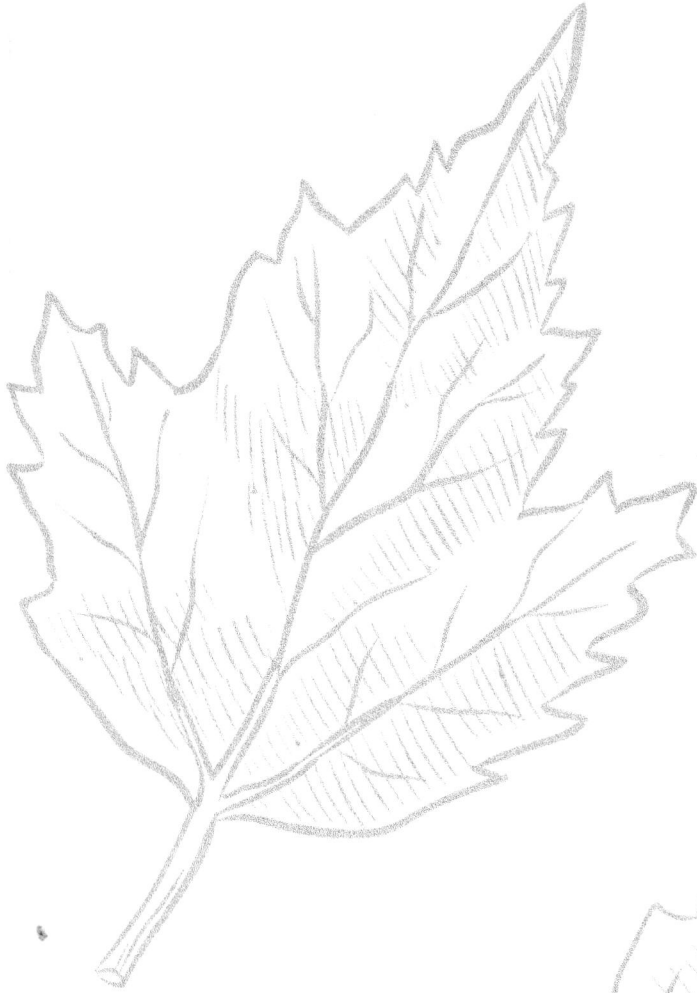

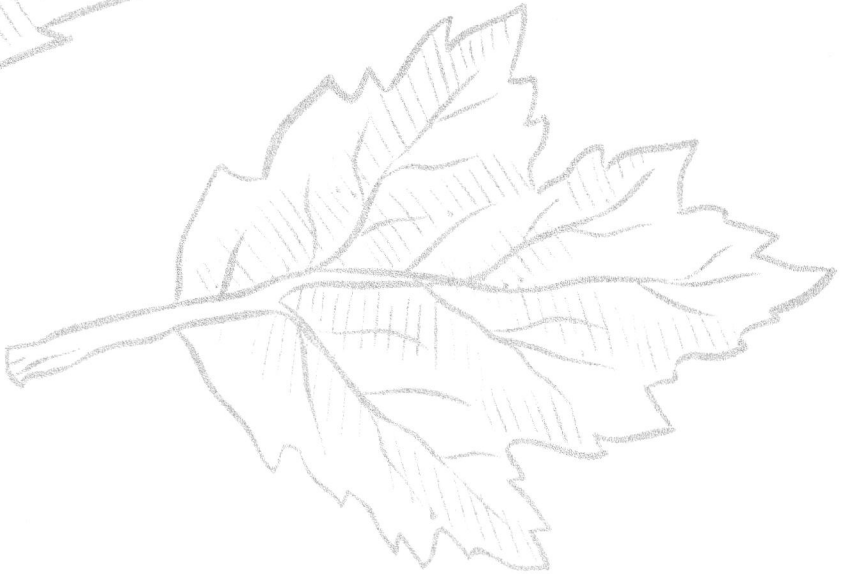

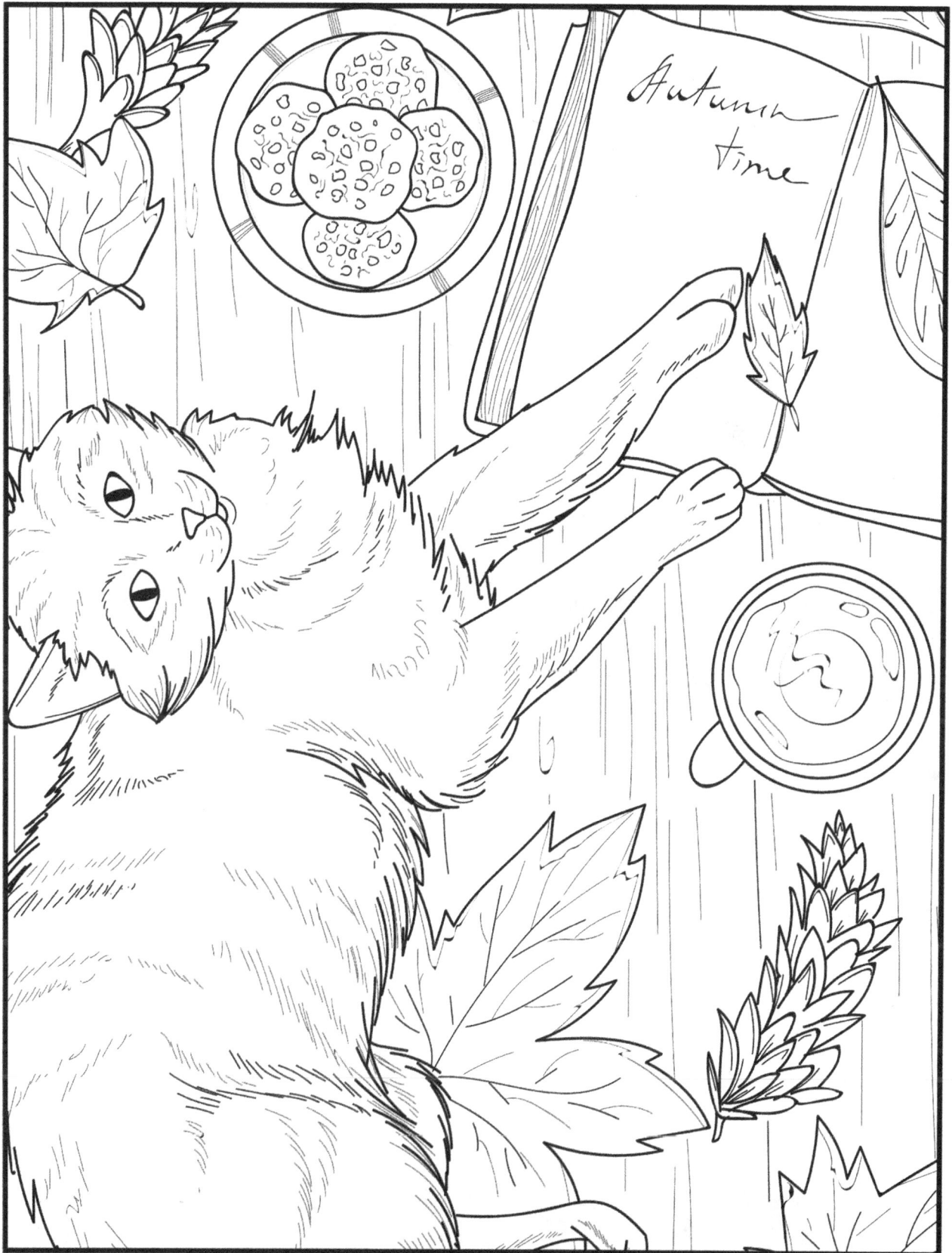
Autumn
time

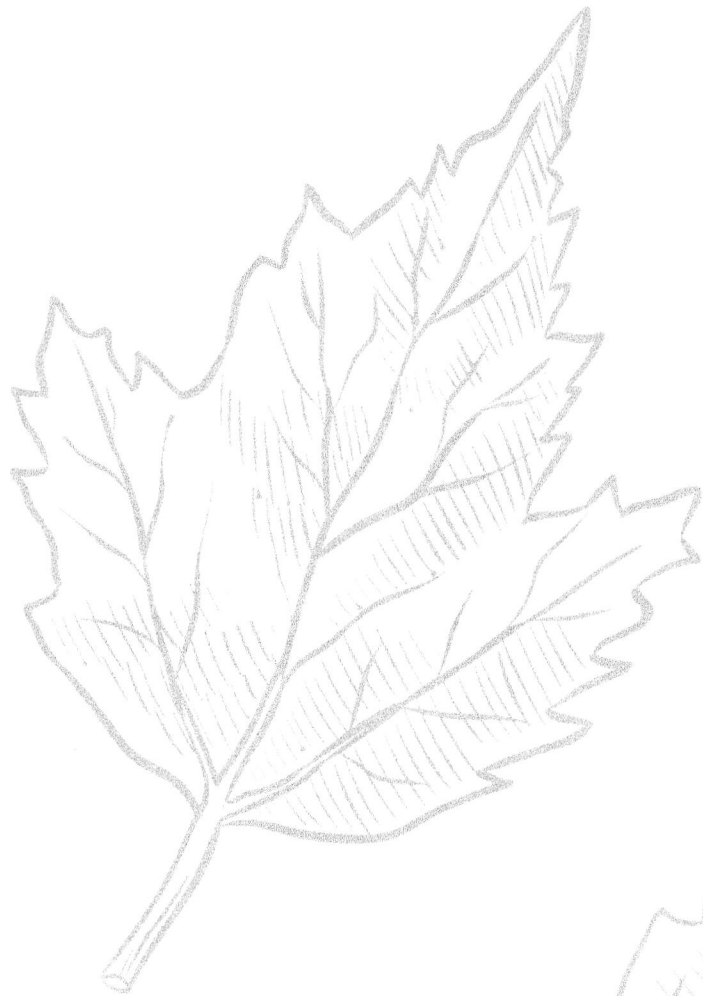

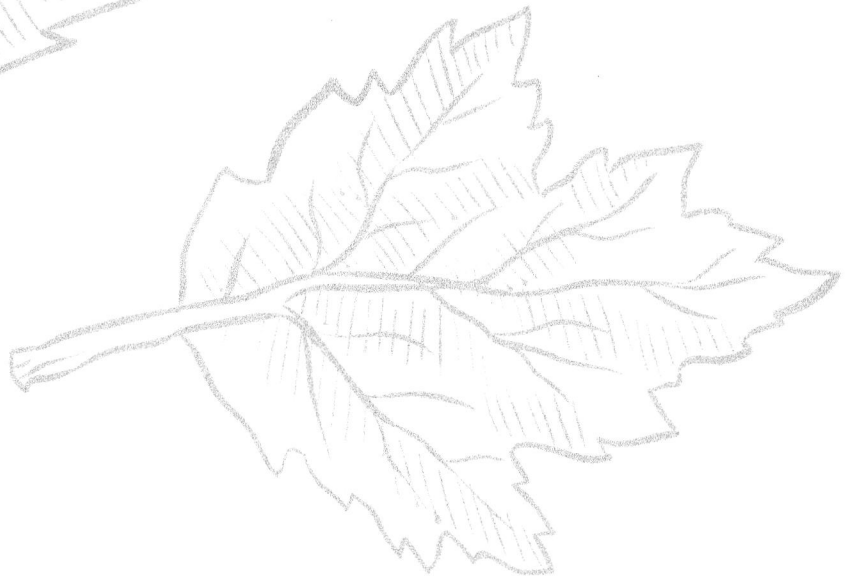

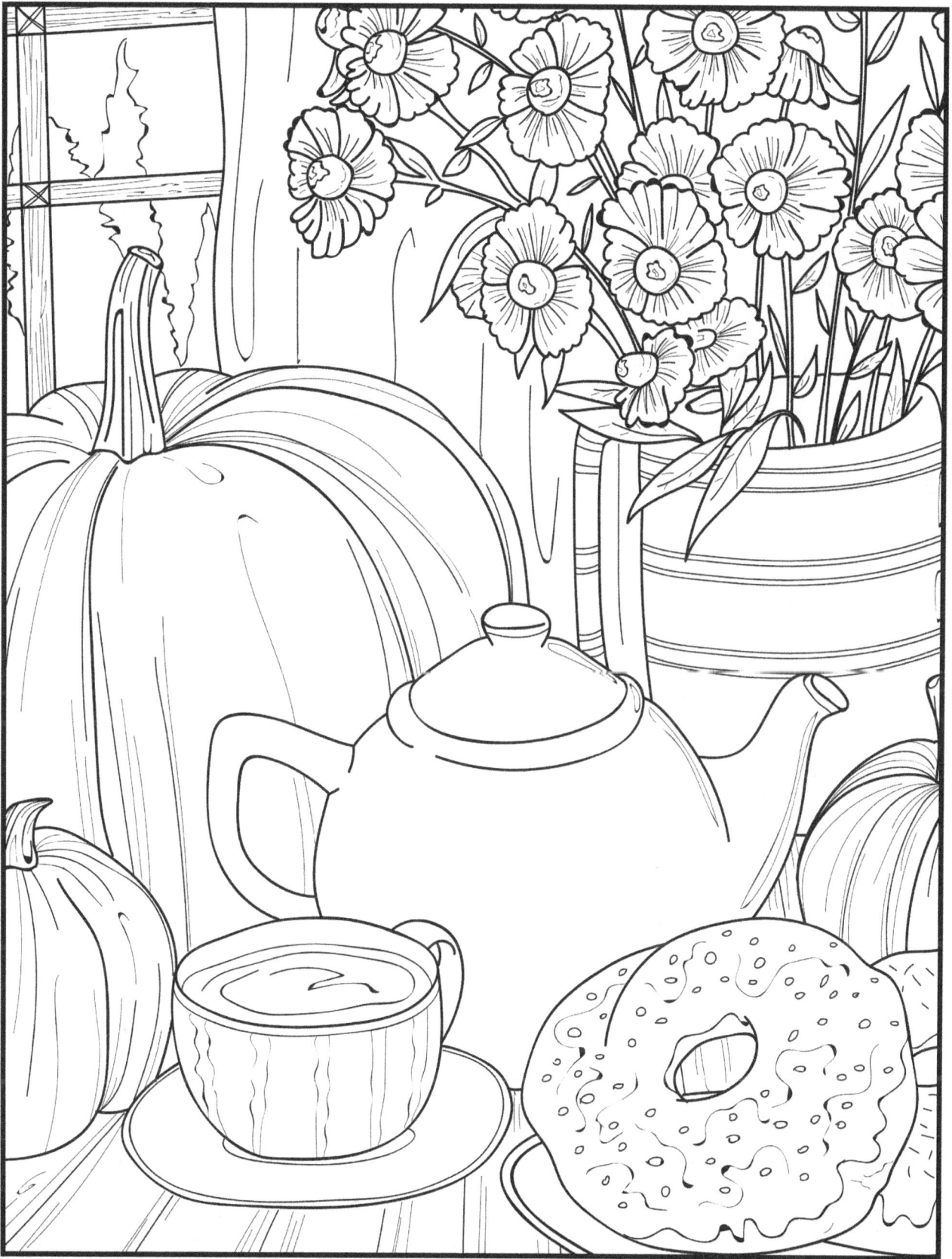

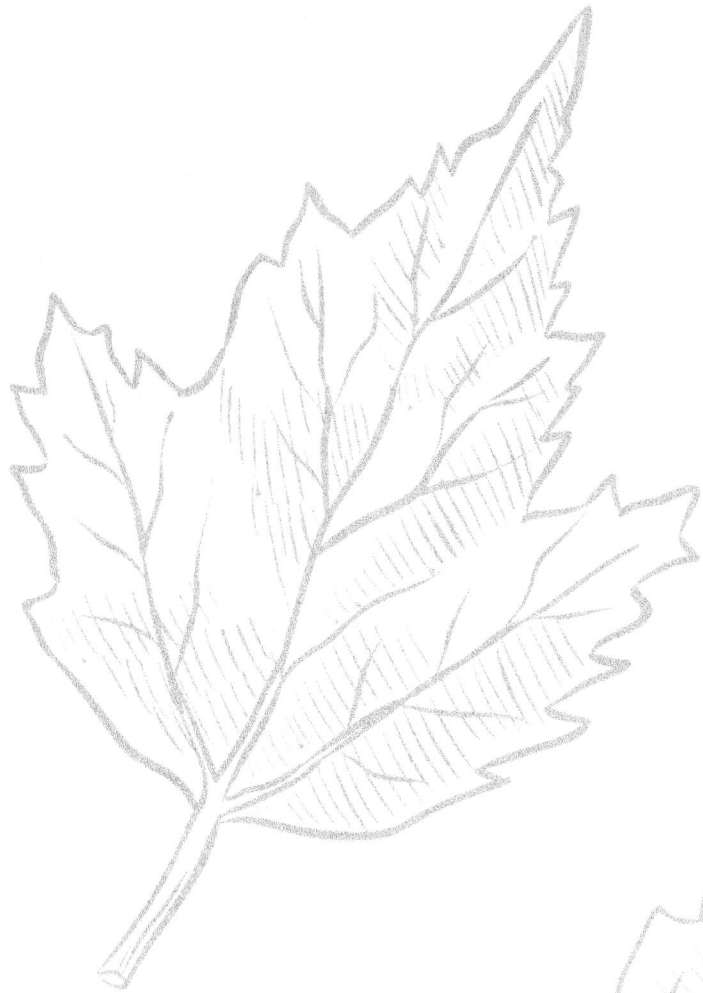

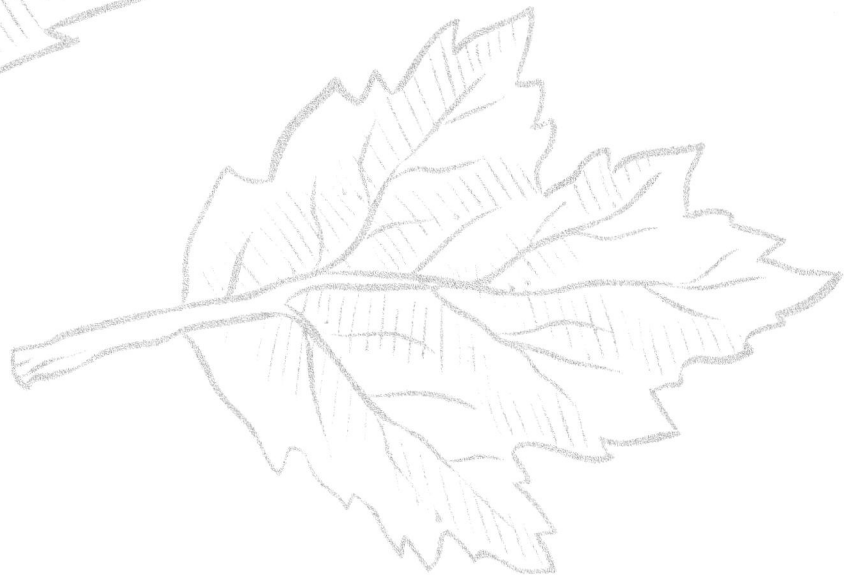

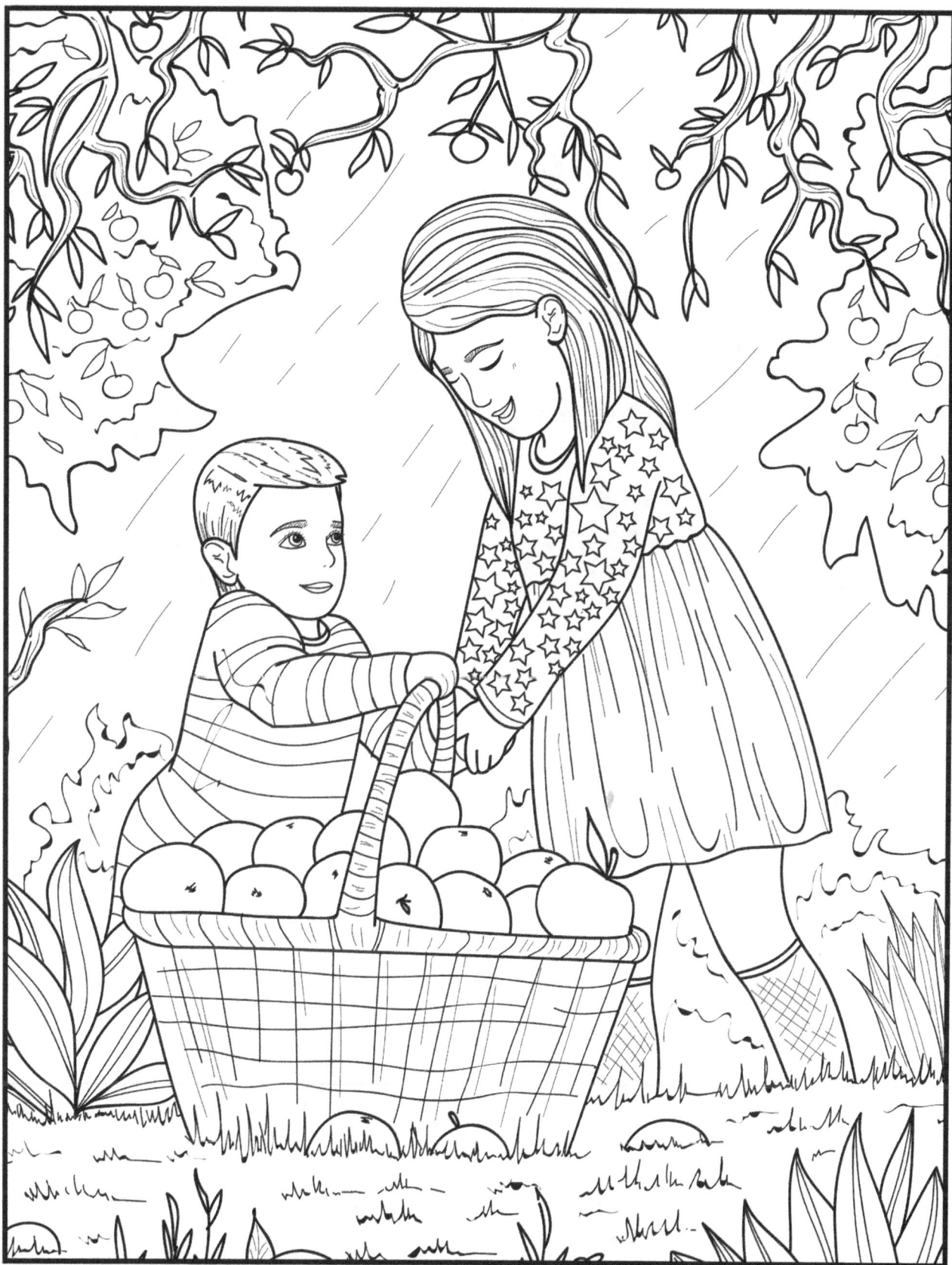

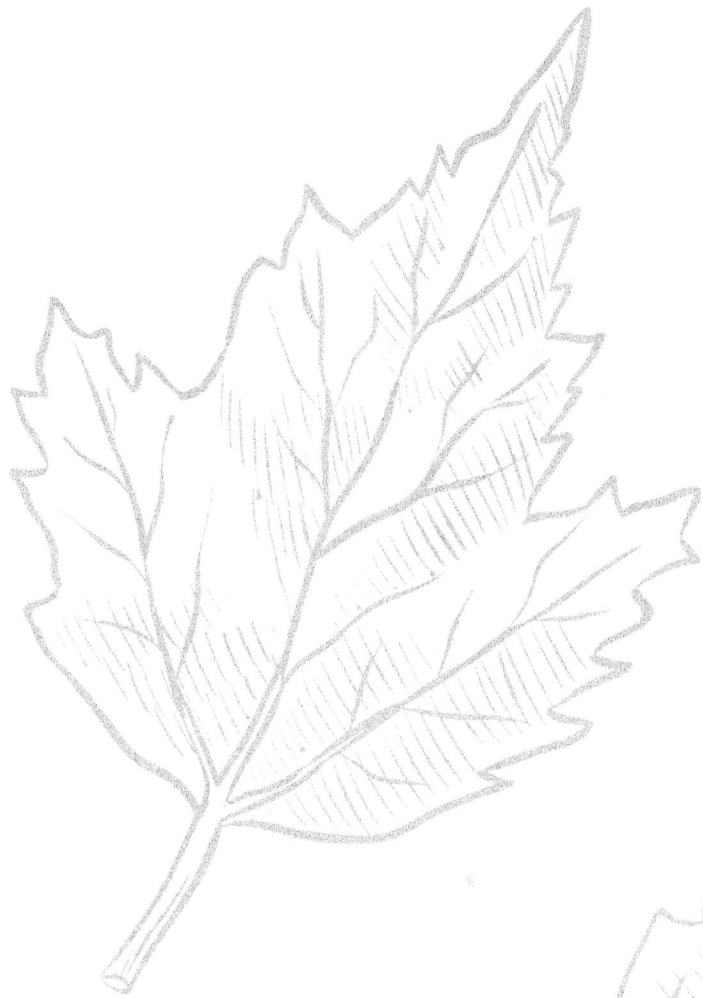

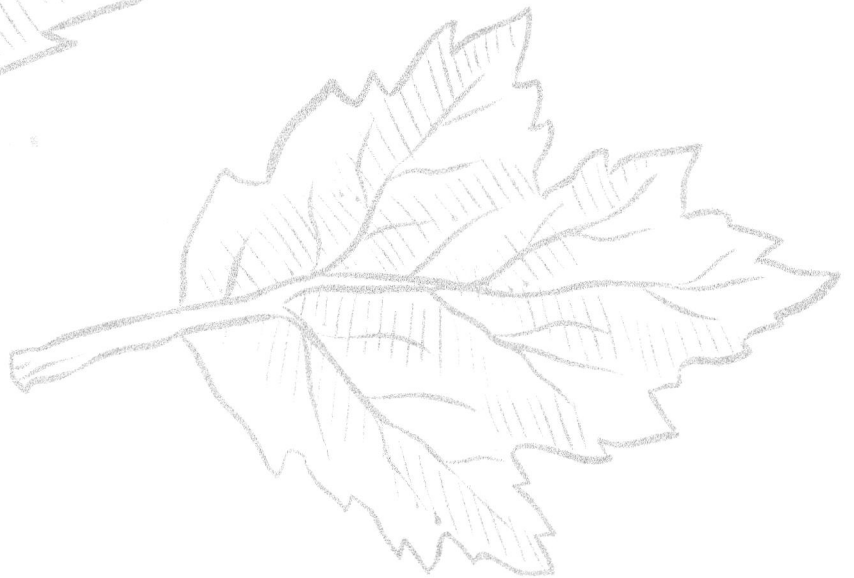

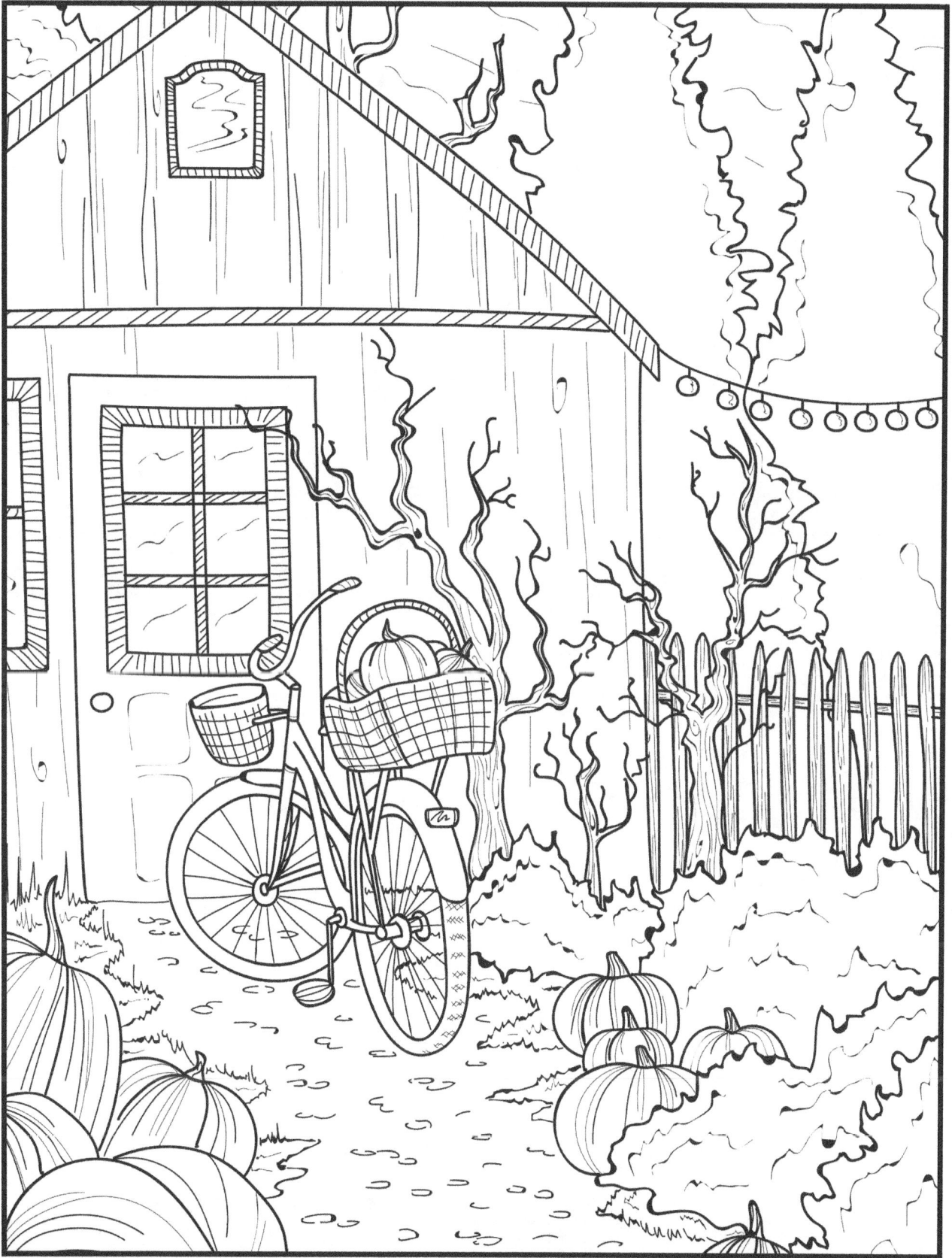

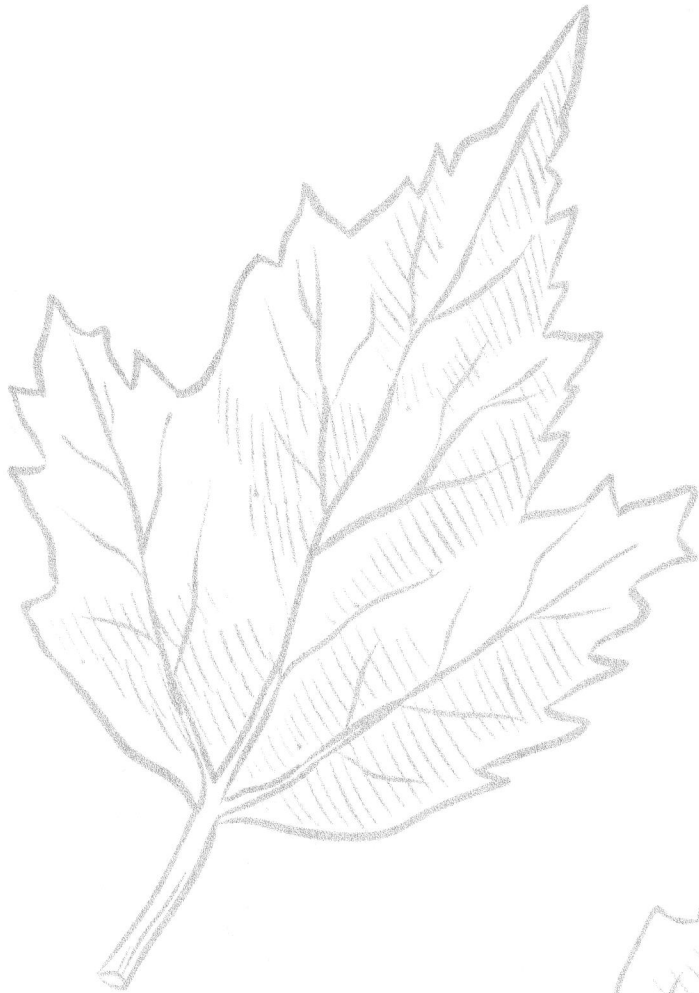

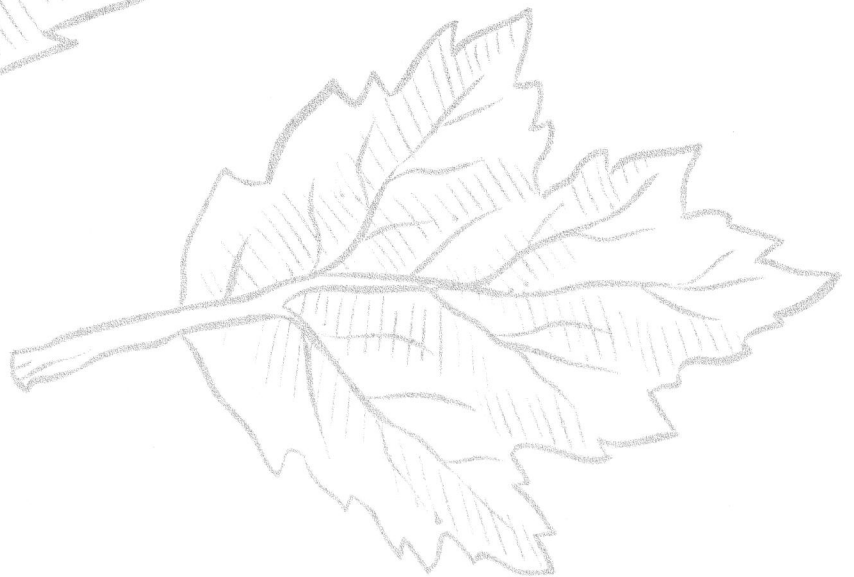

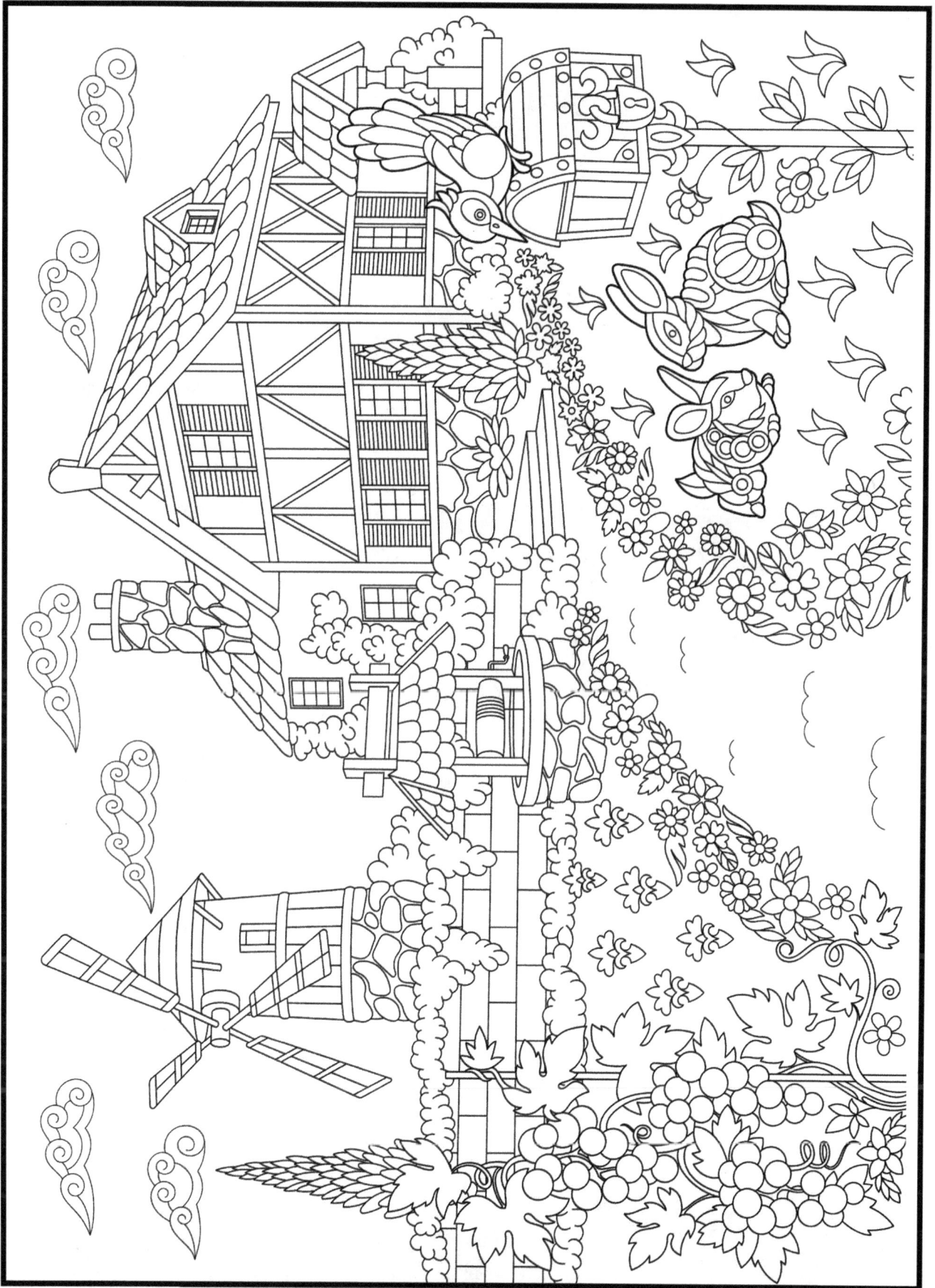

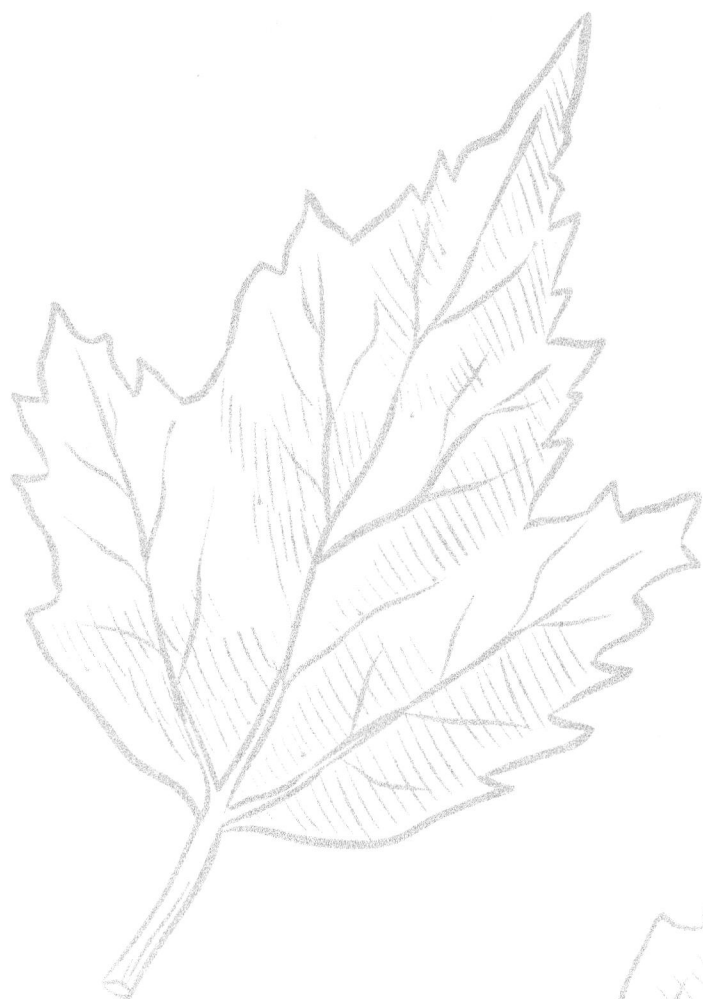

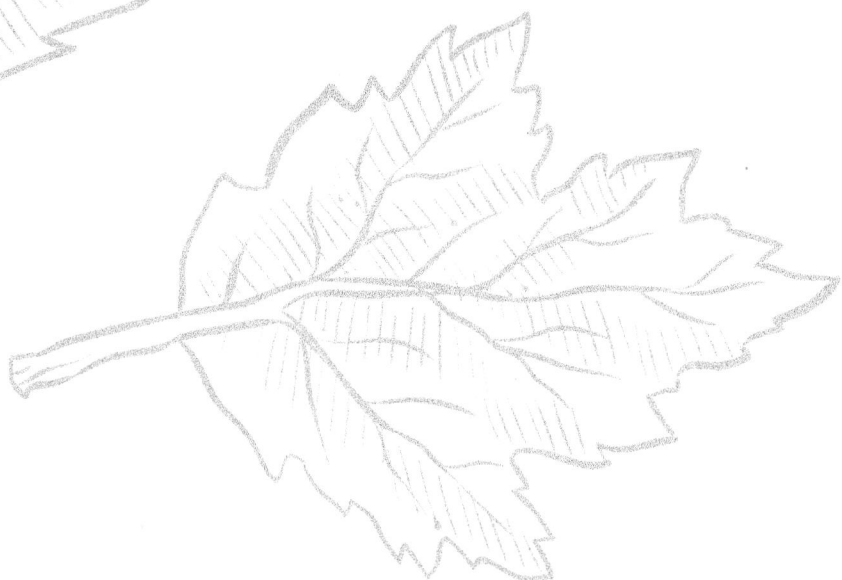

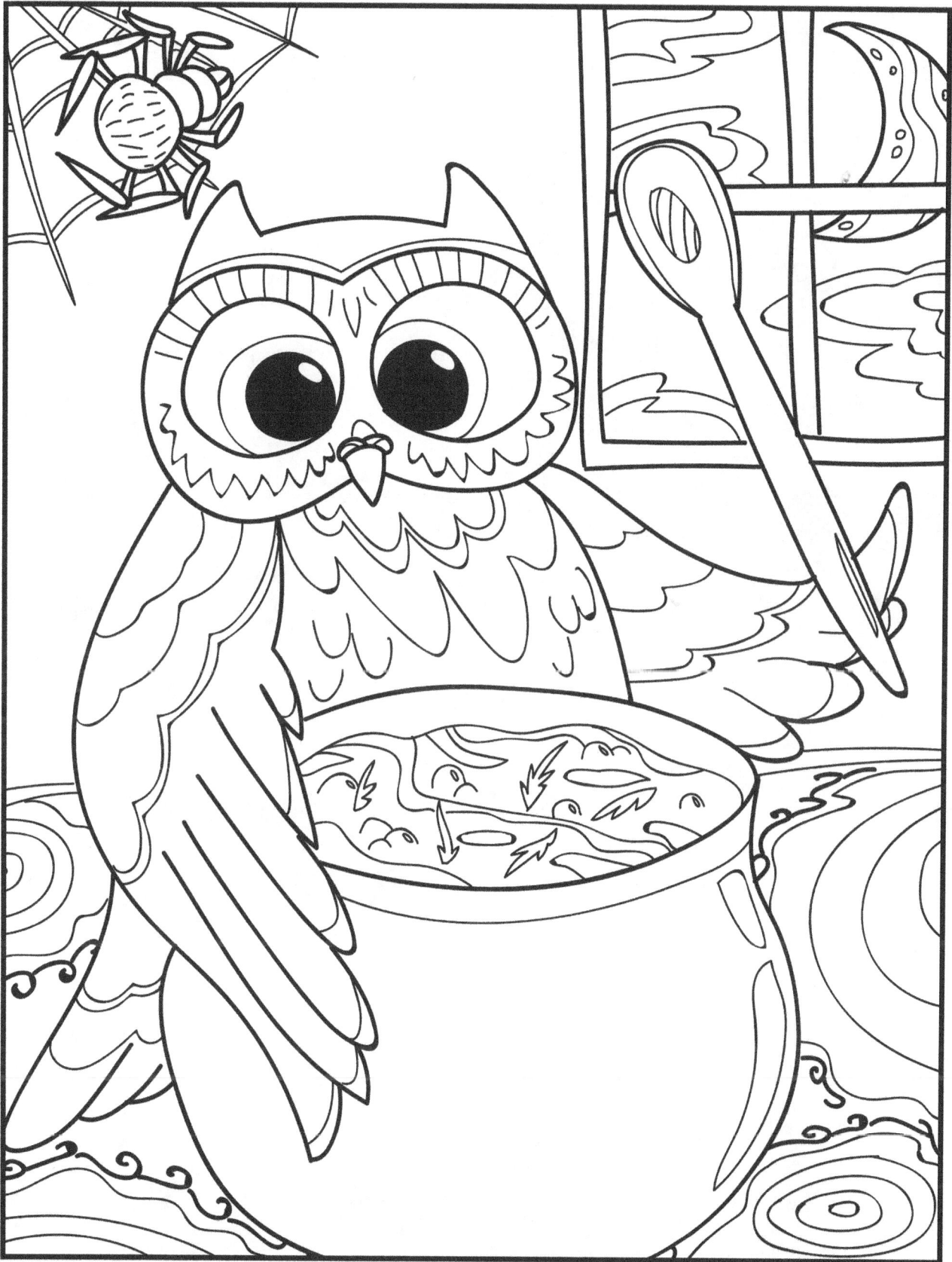

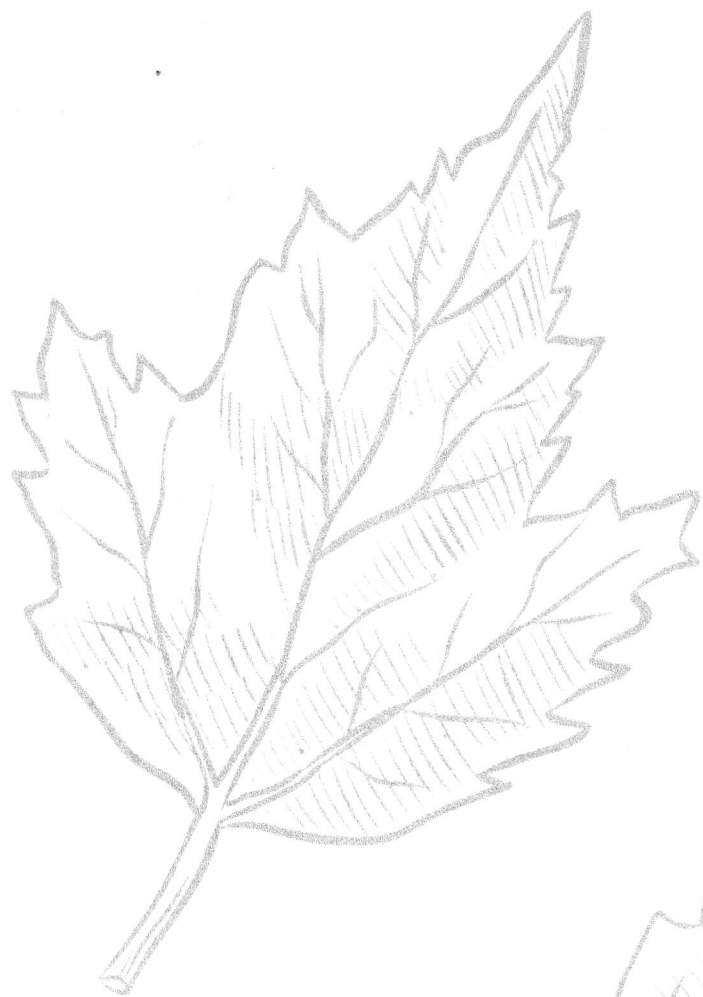

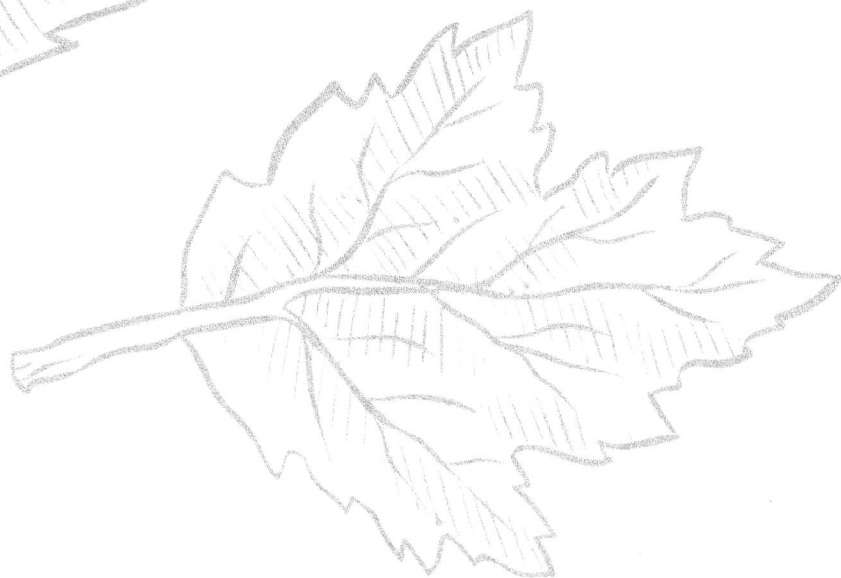

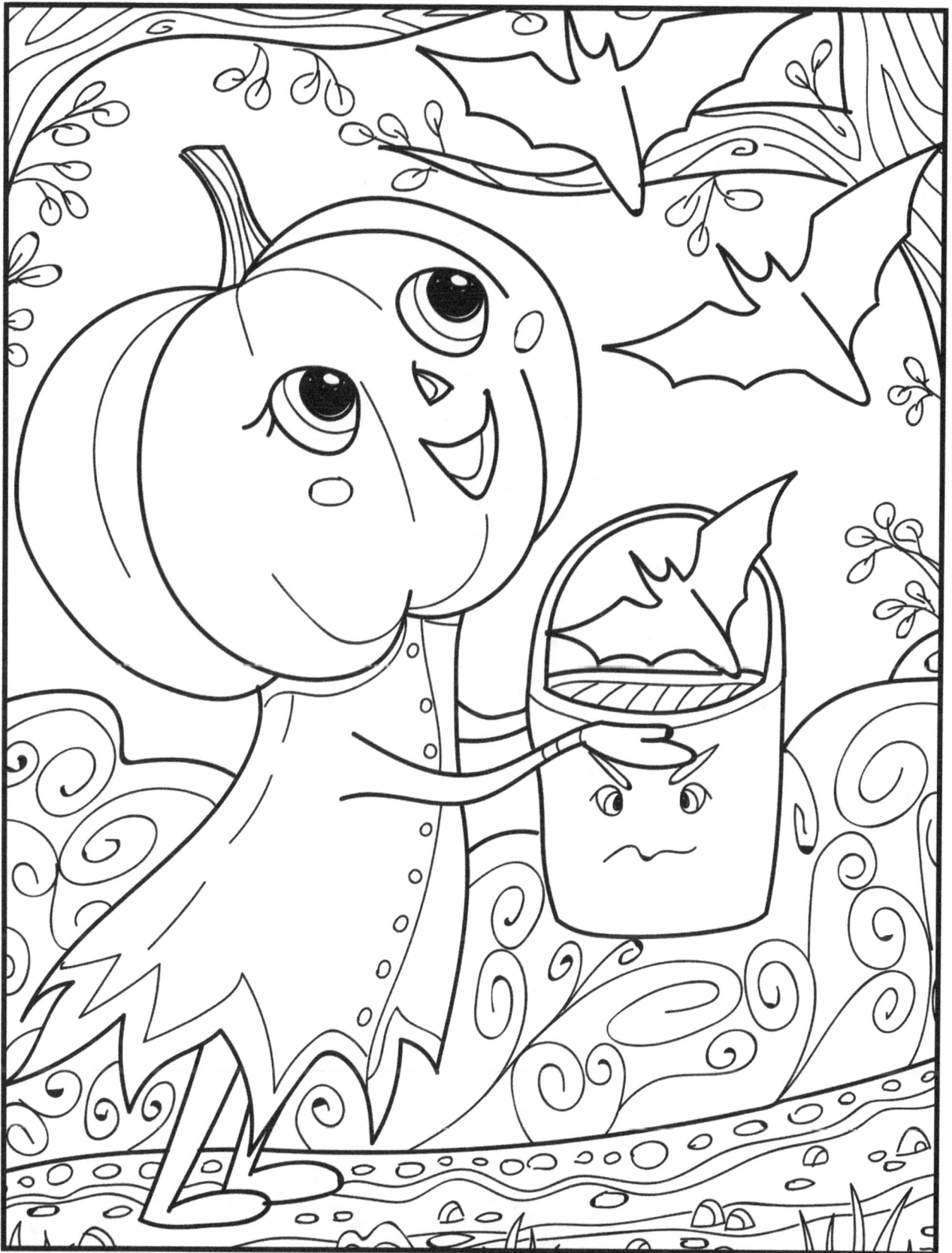

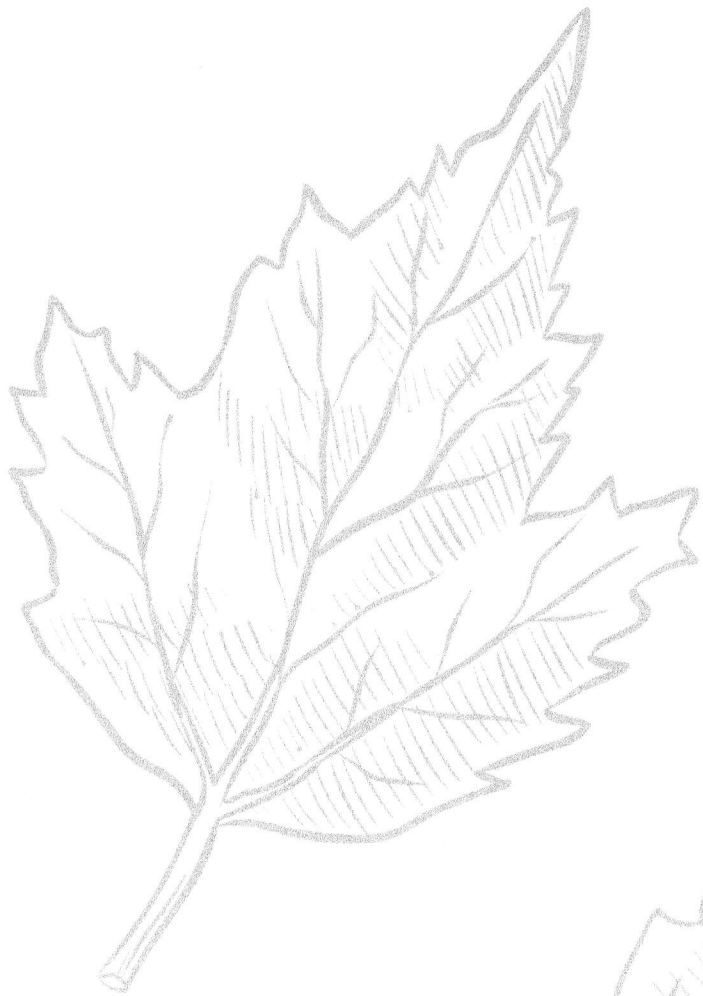

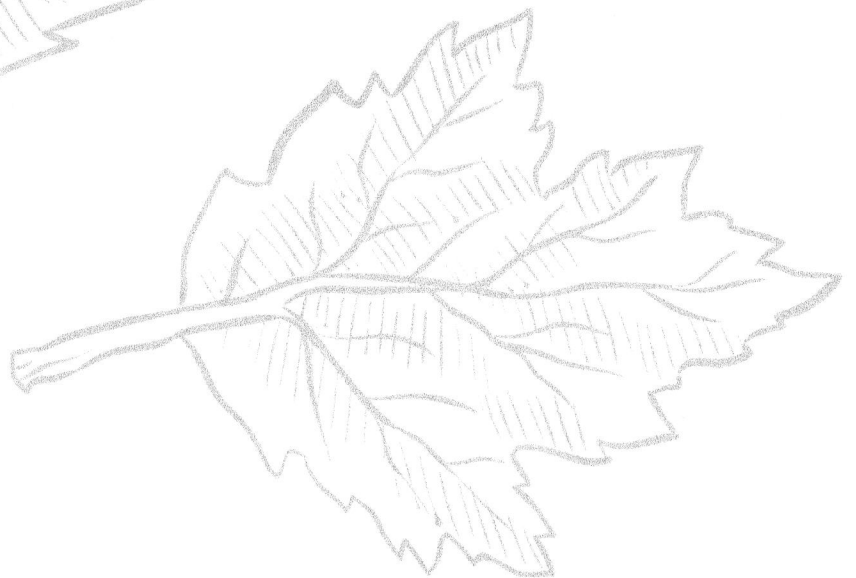

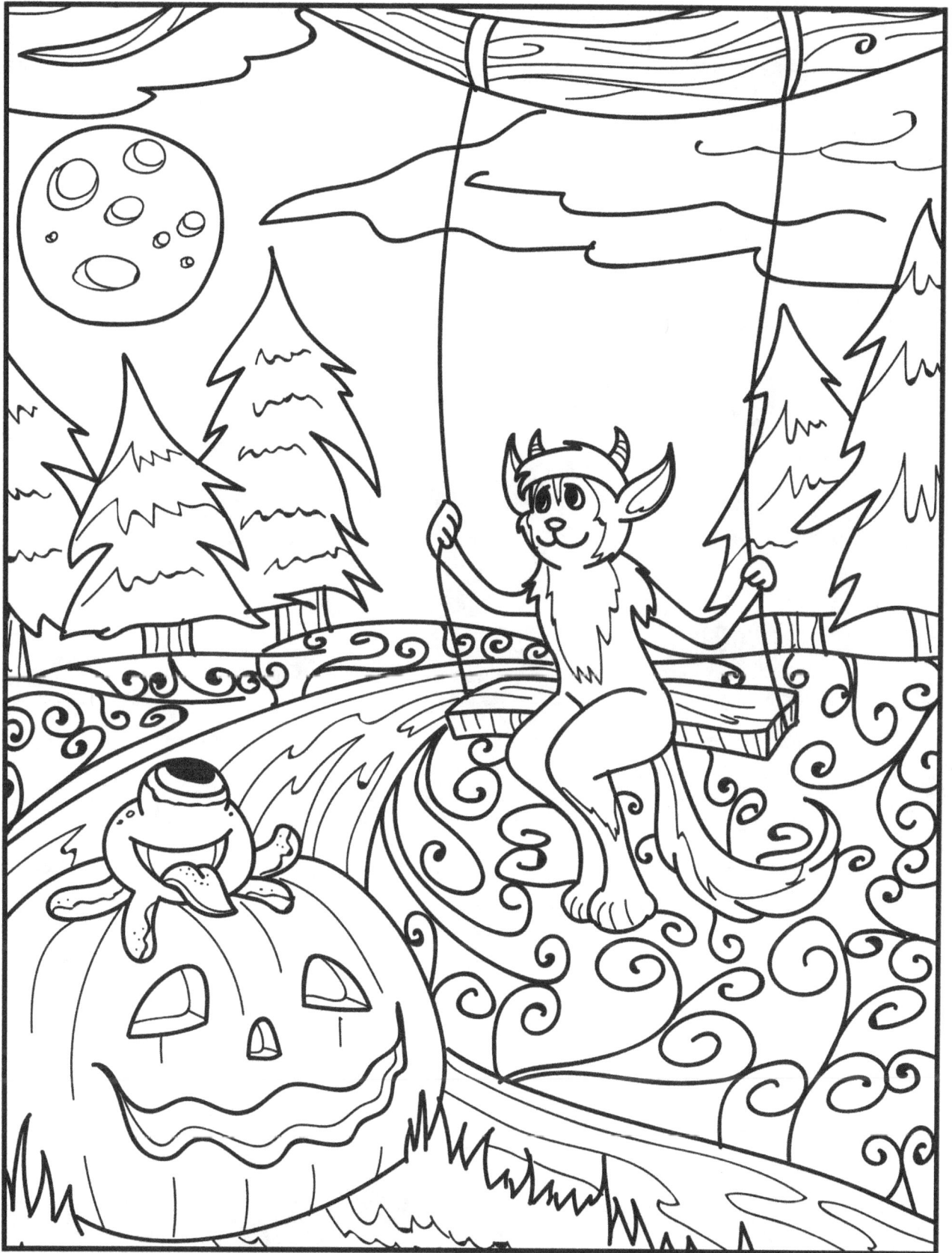

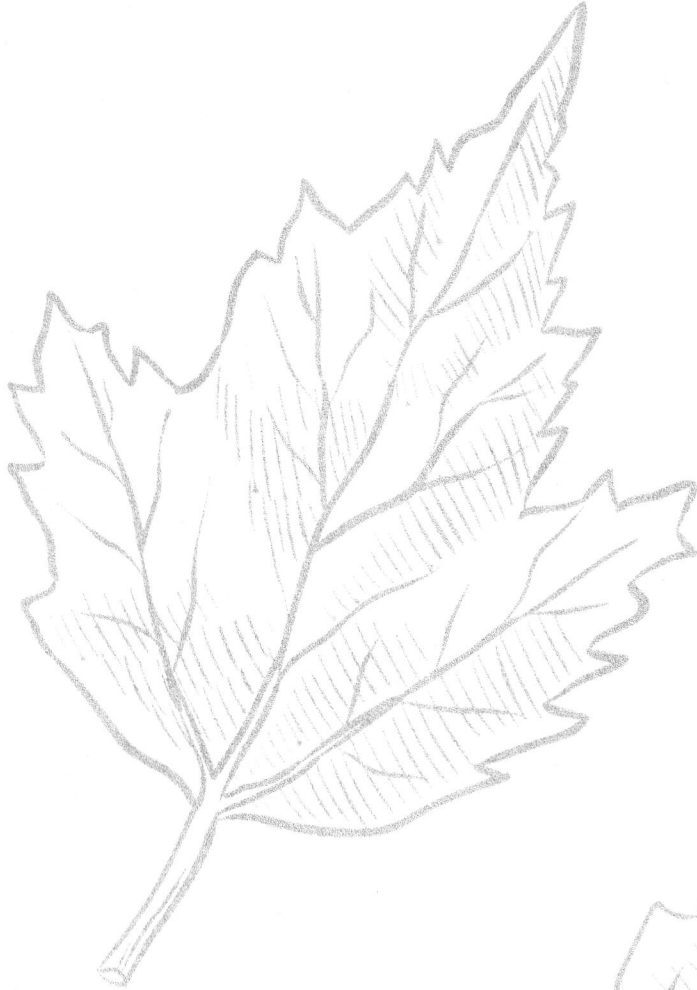

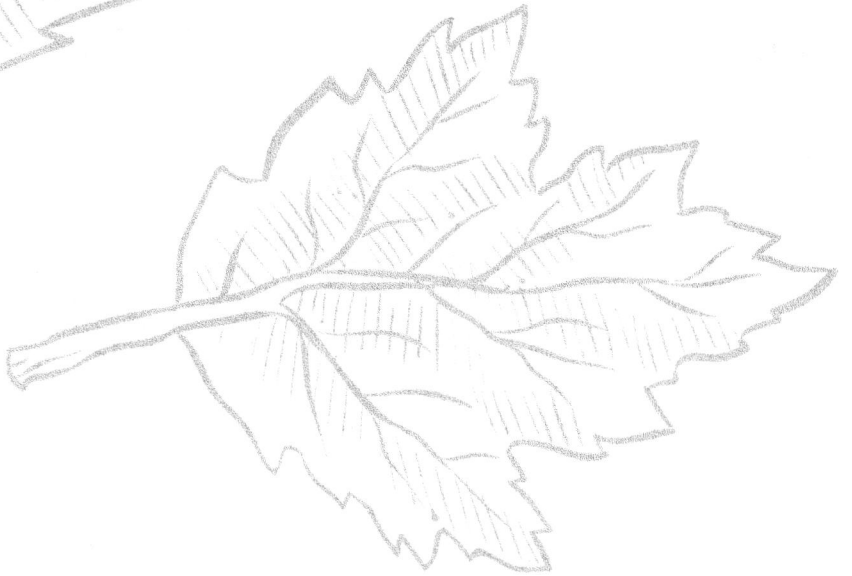

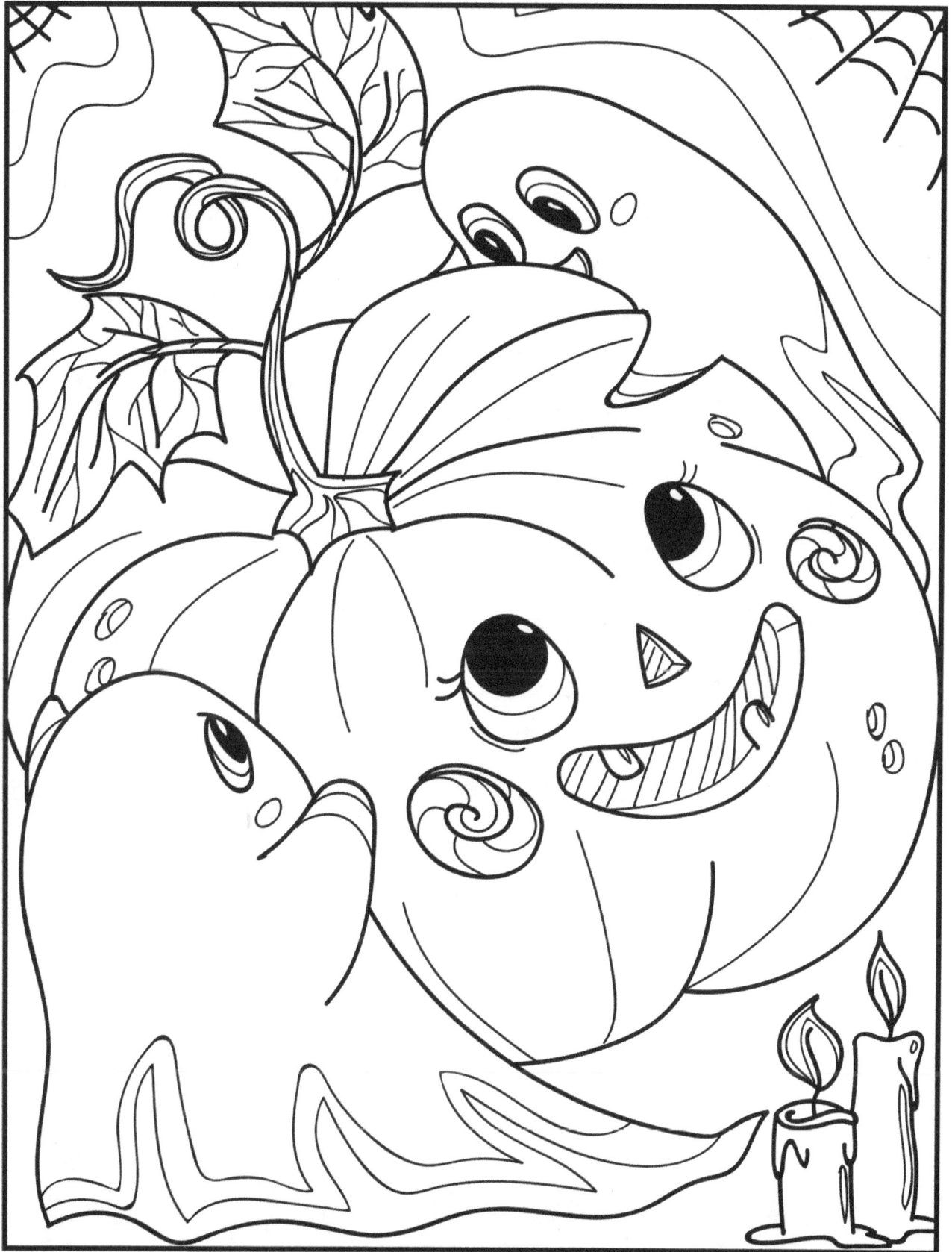

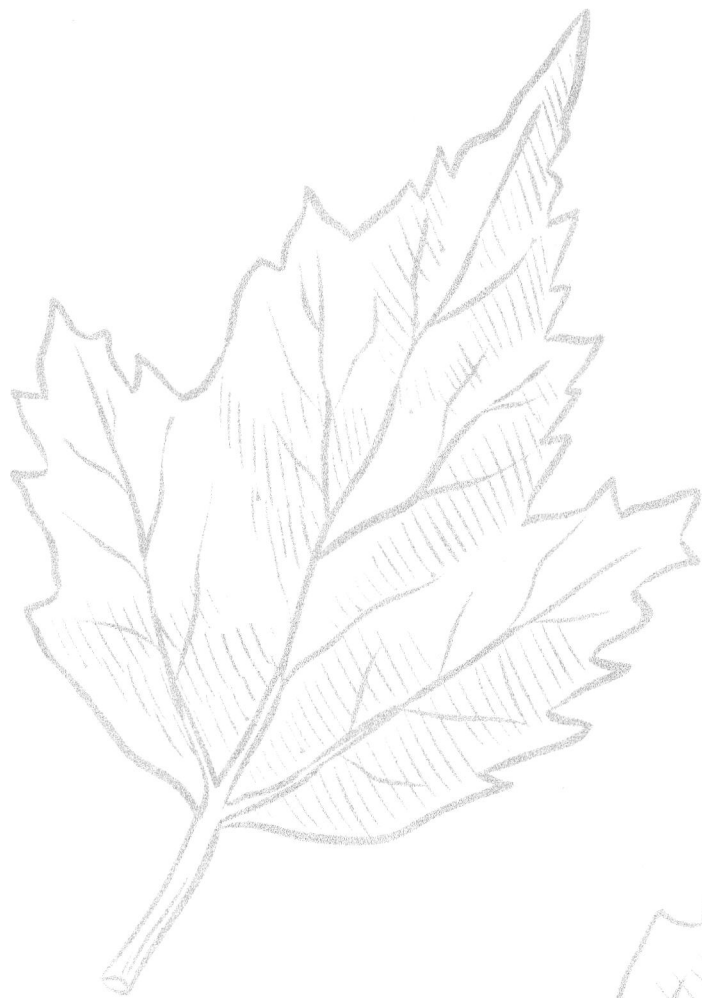

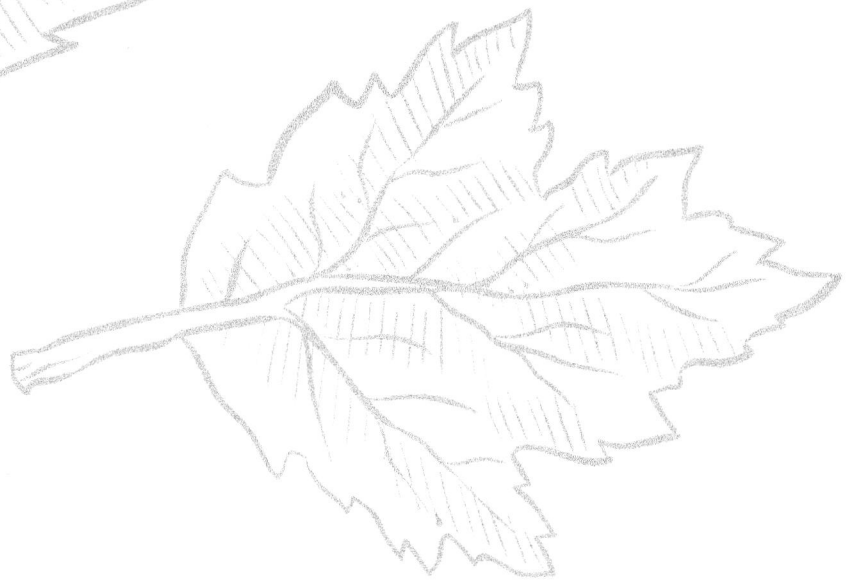

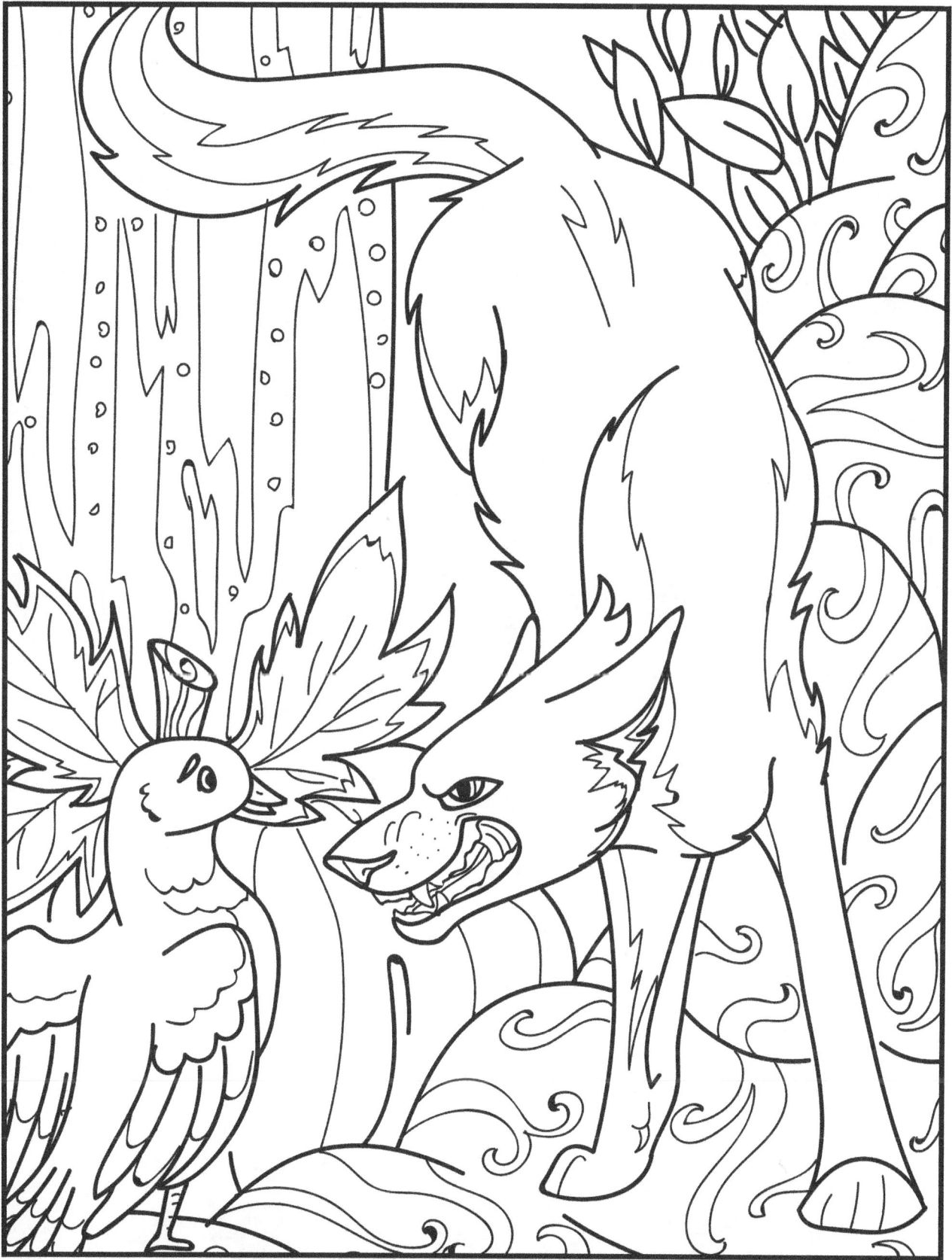

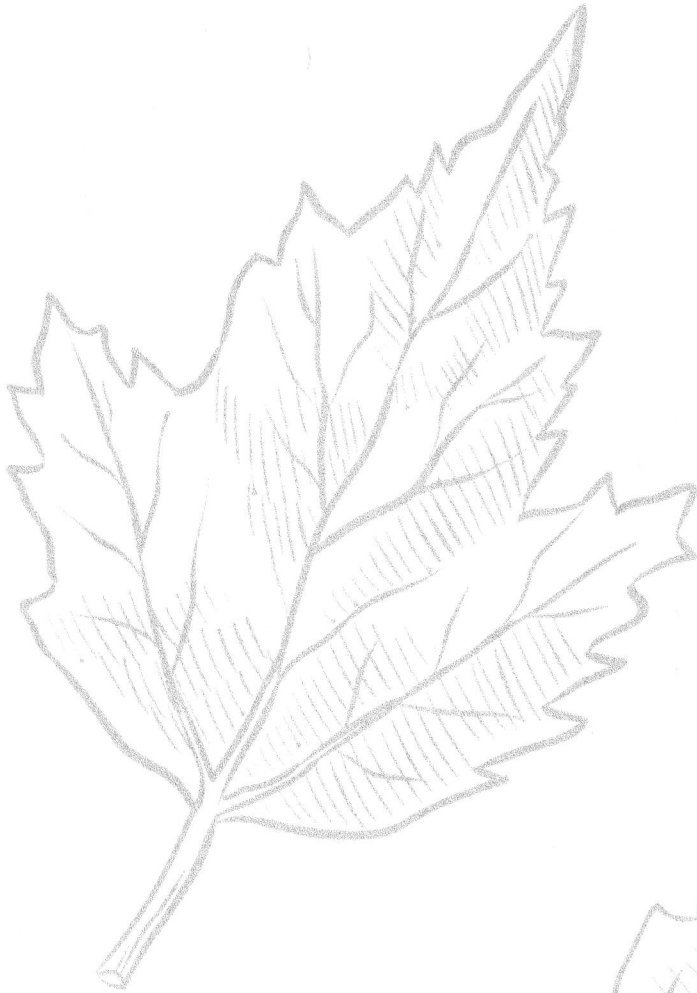

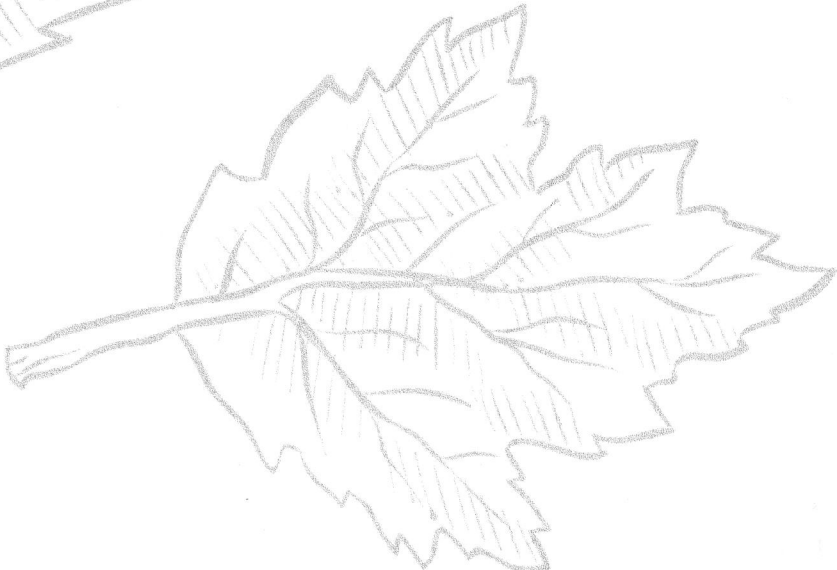

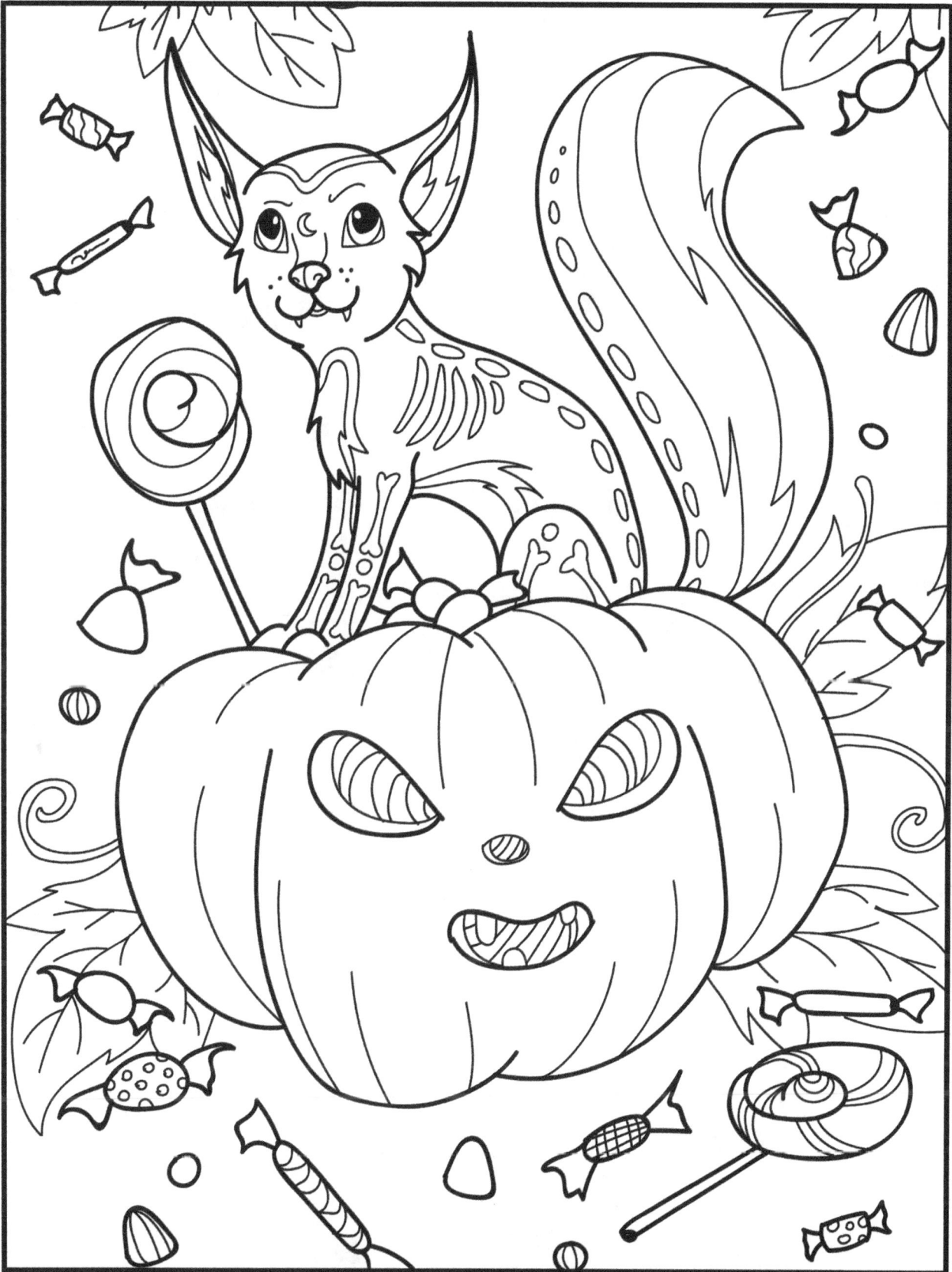

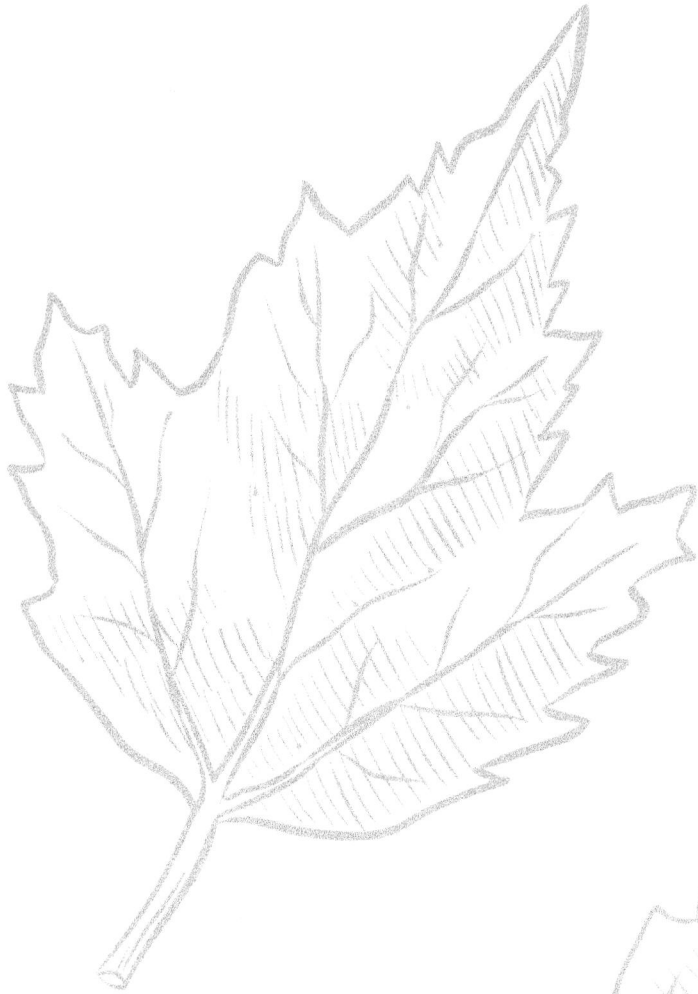

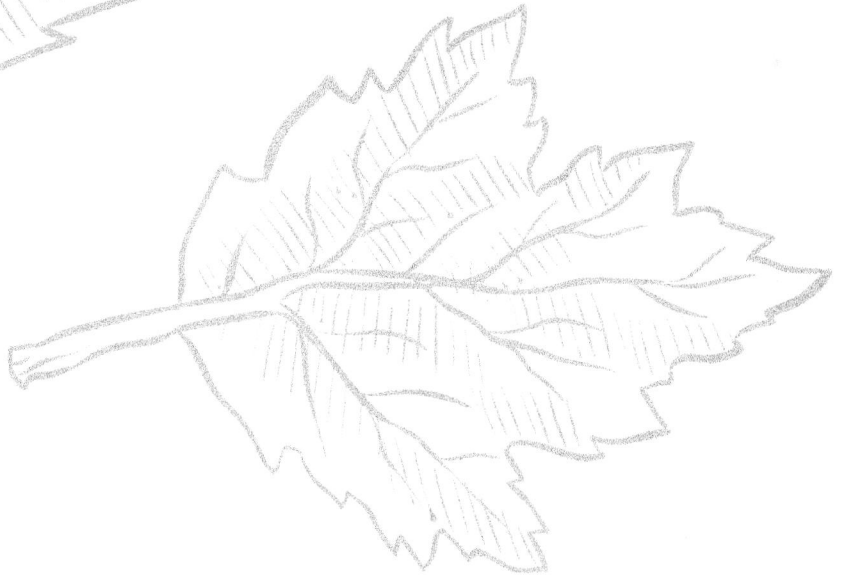

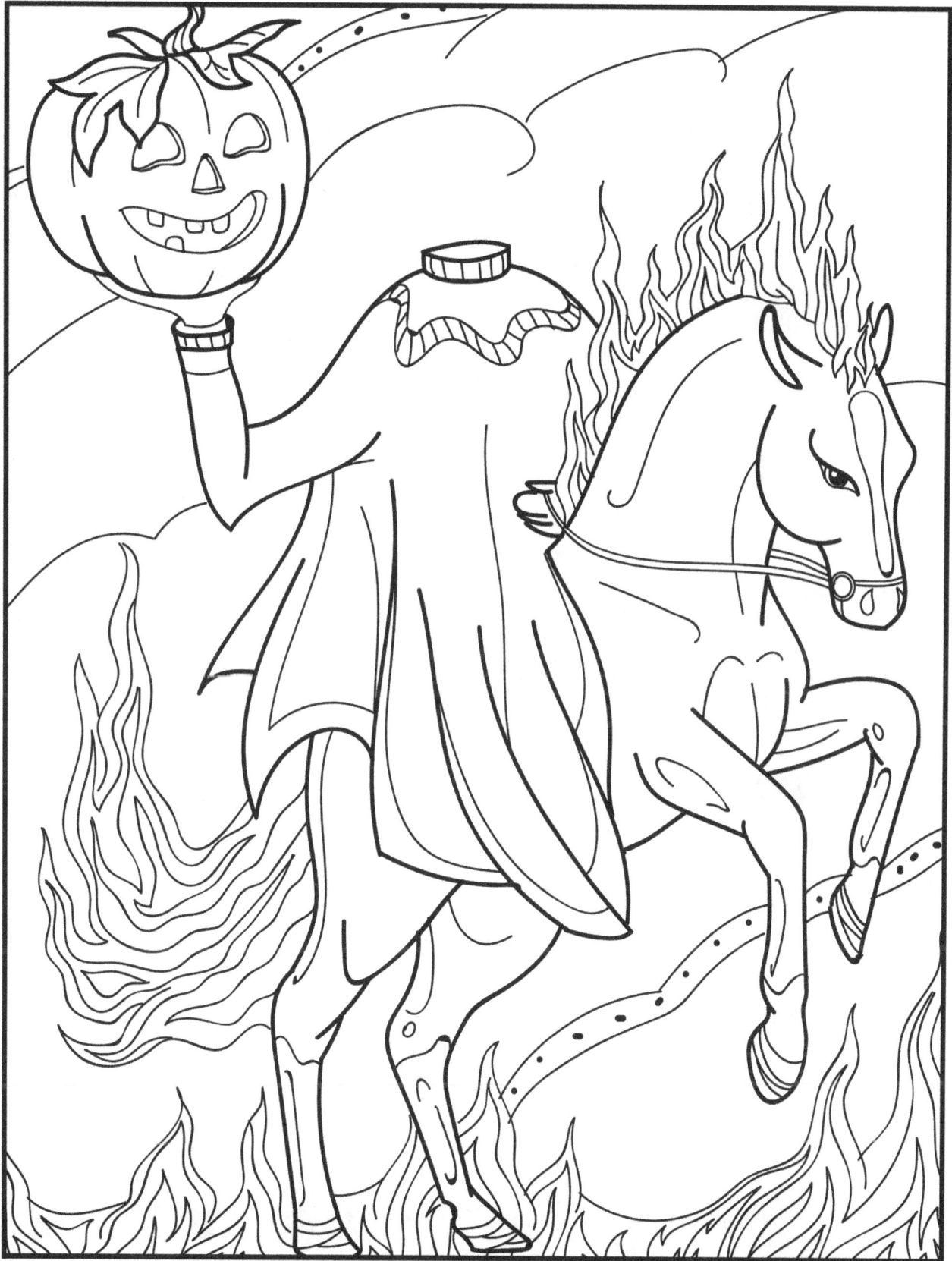

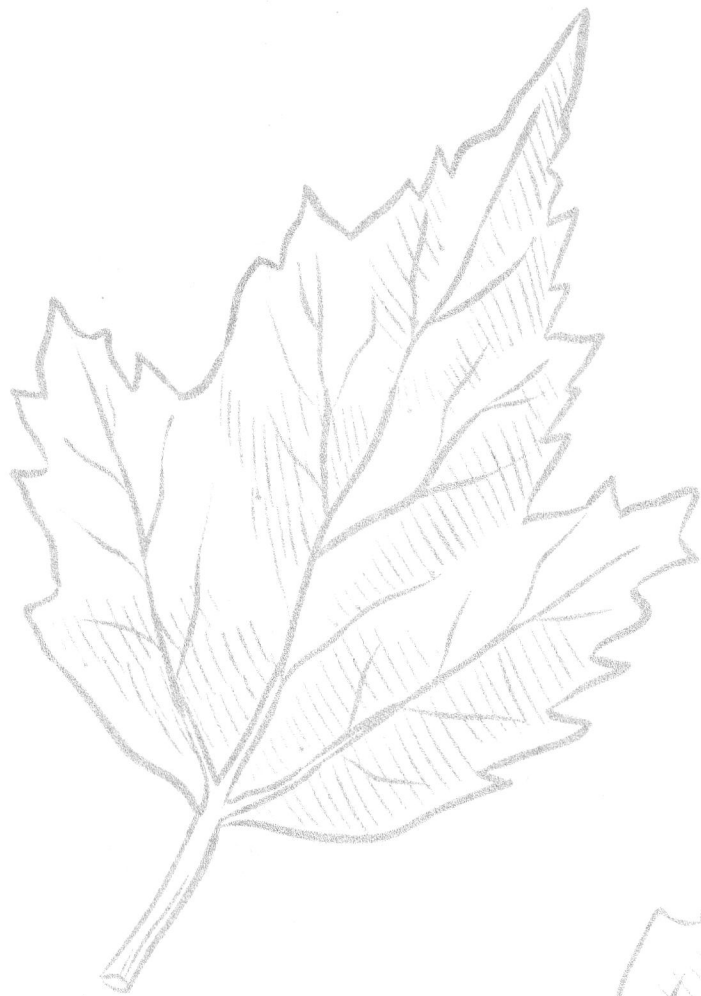

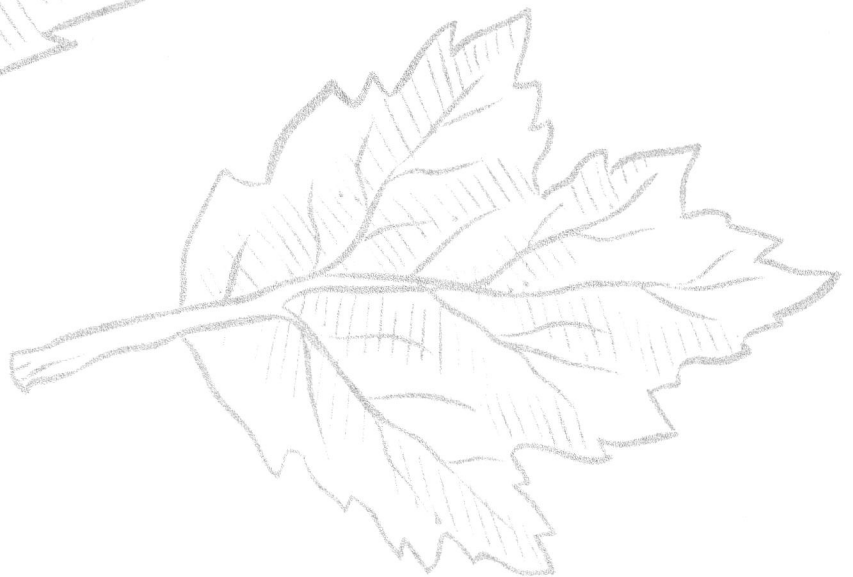

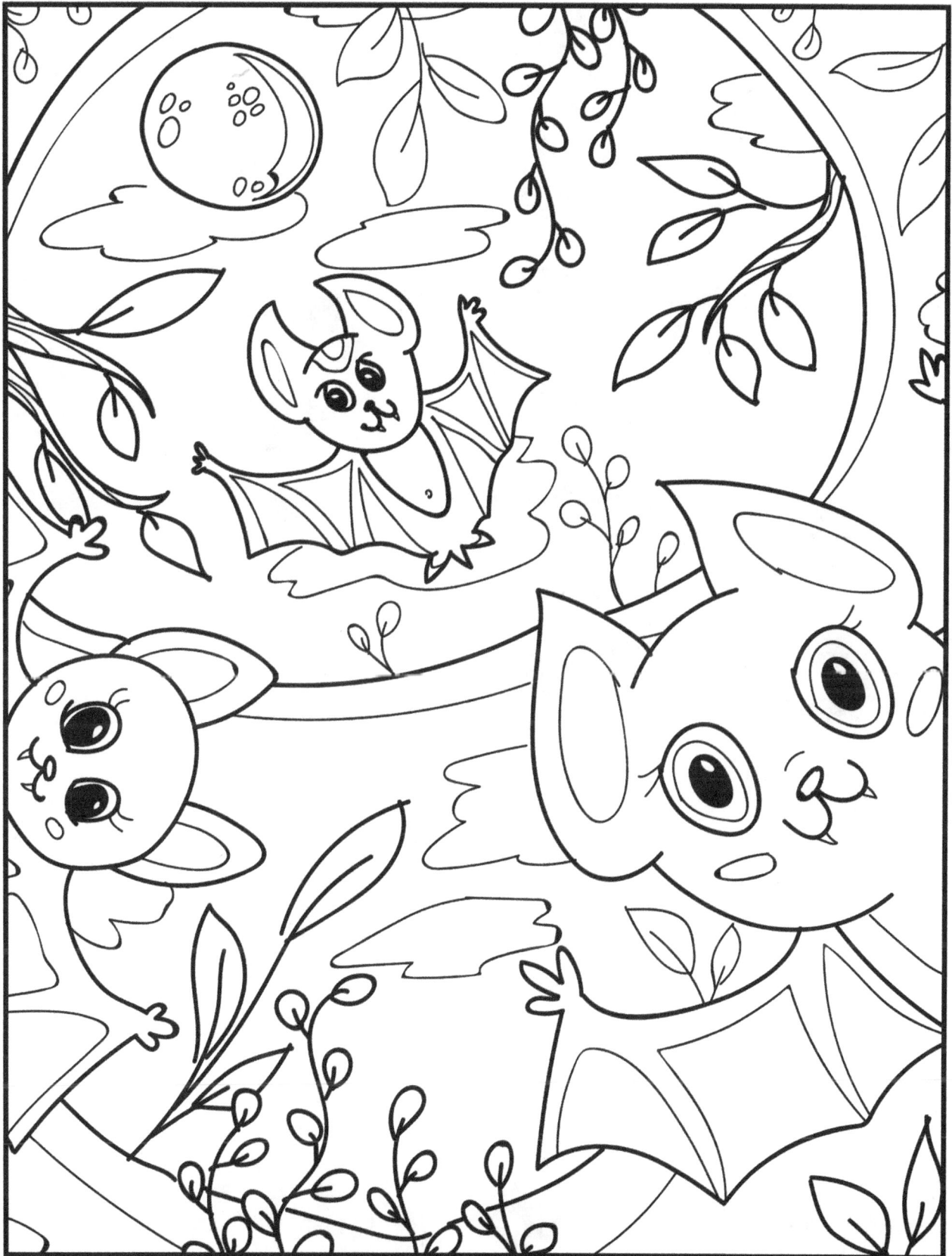

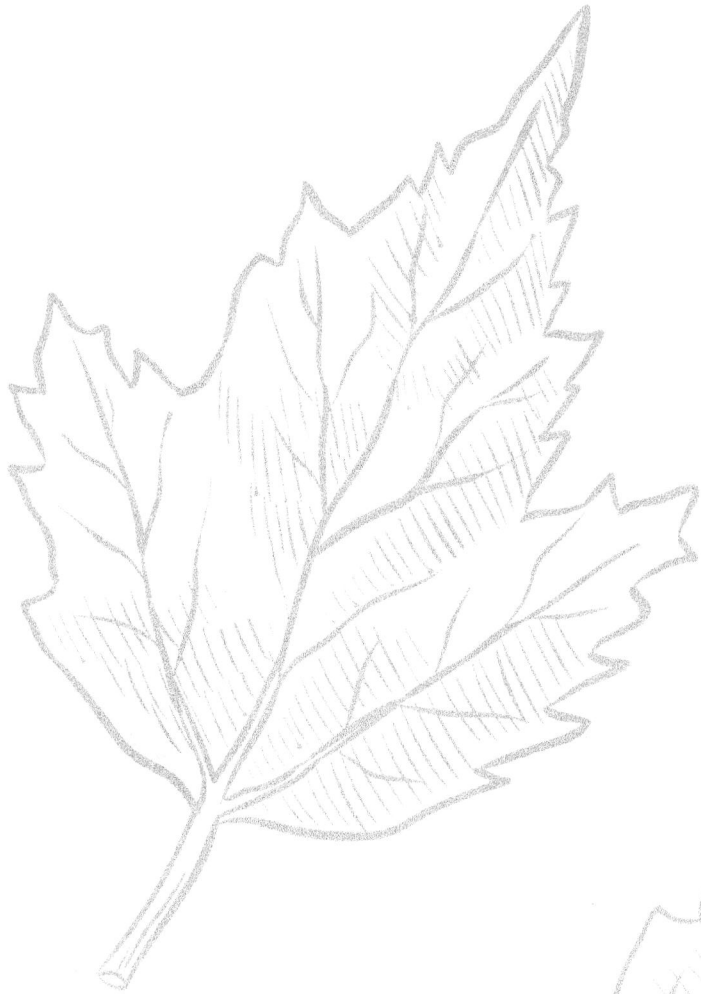

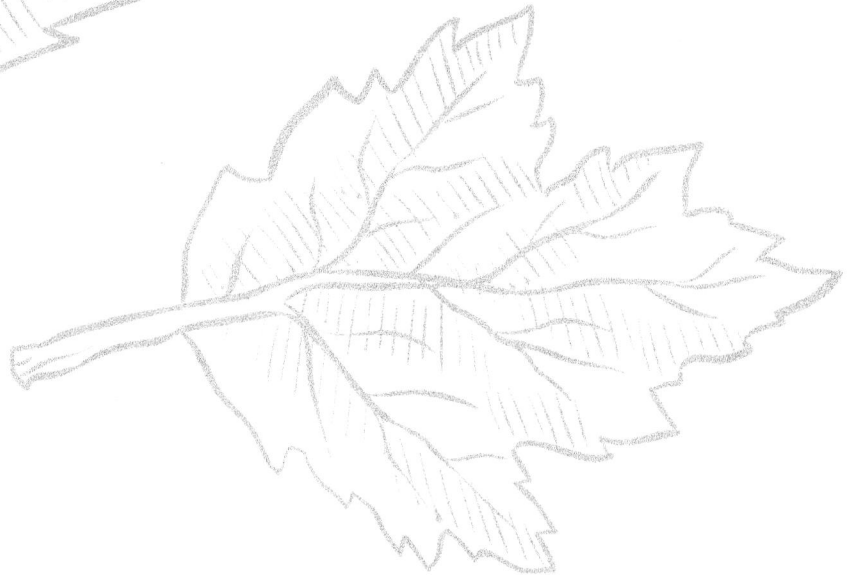

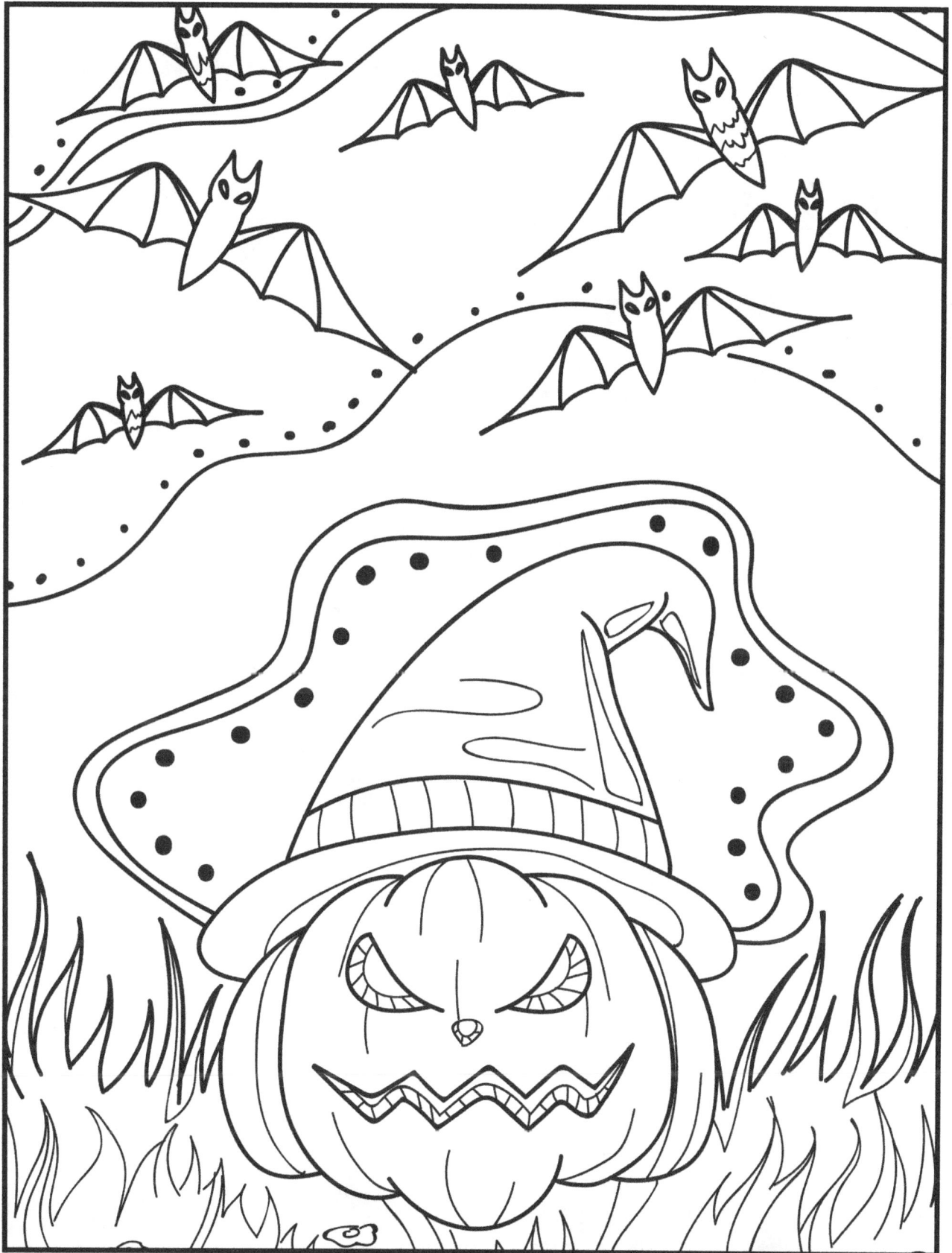

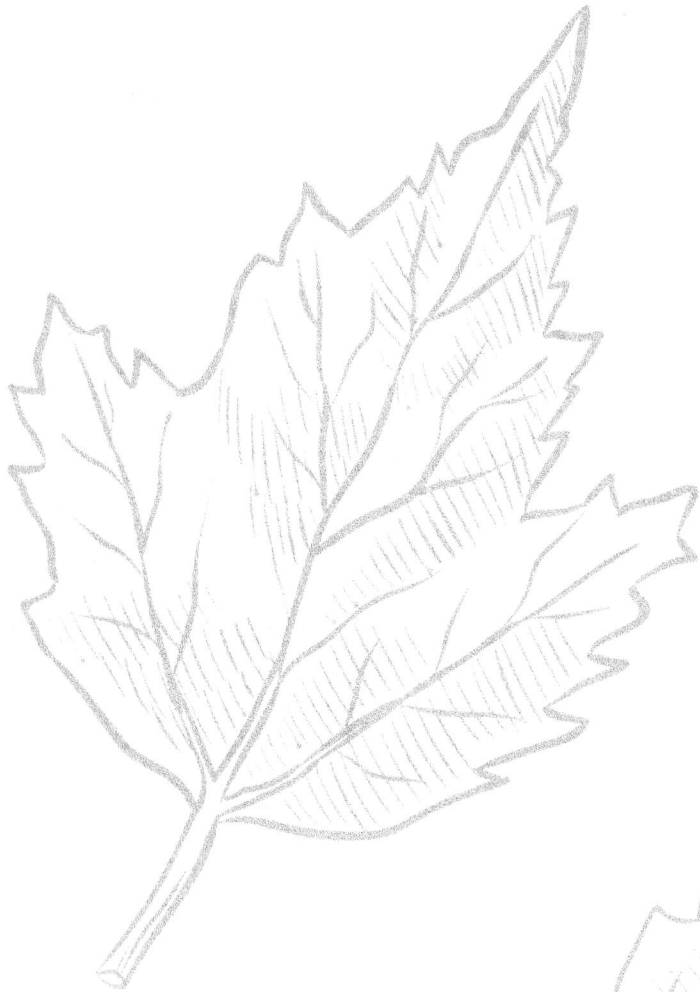

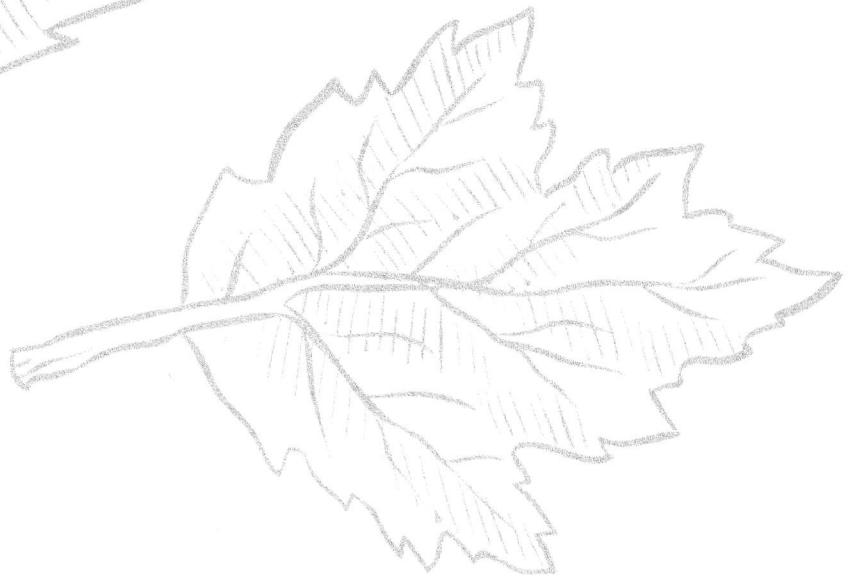

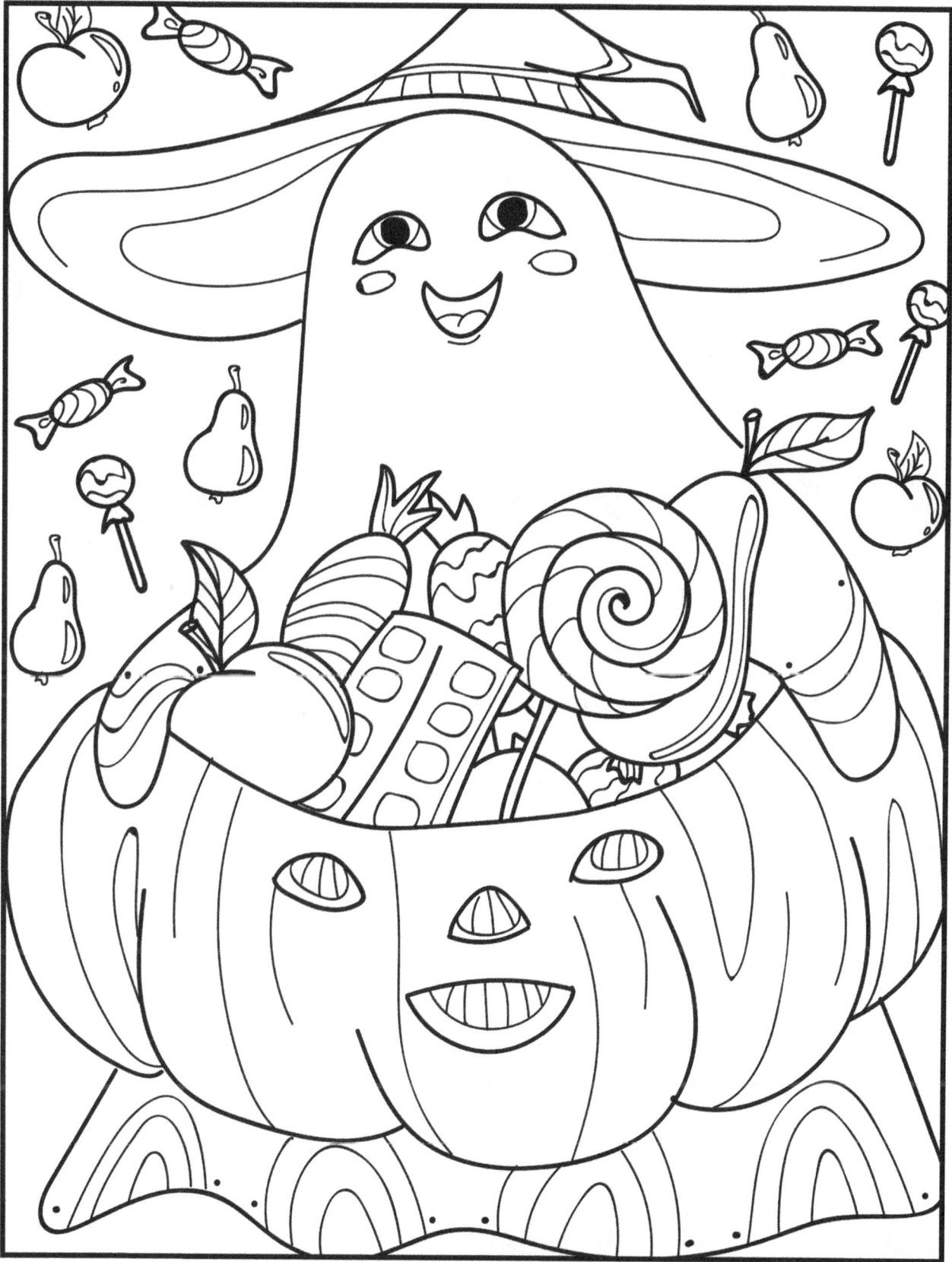

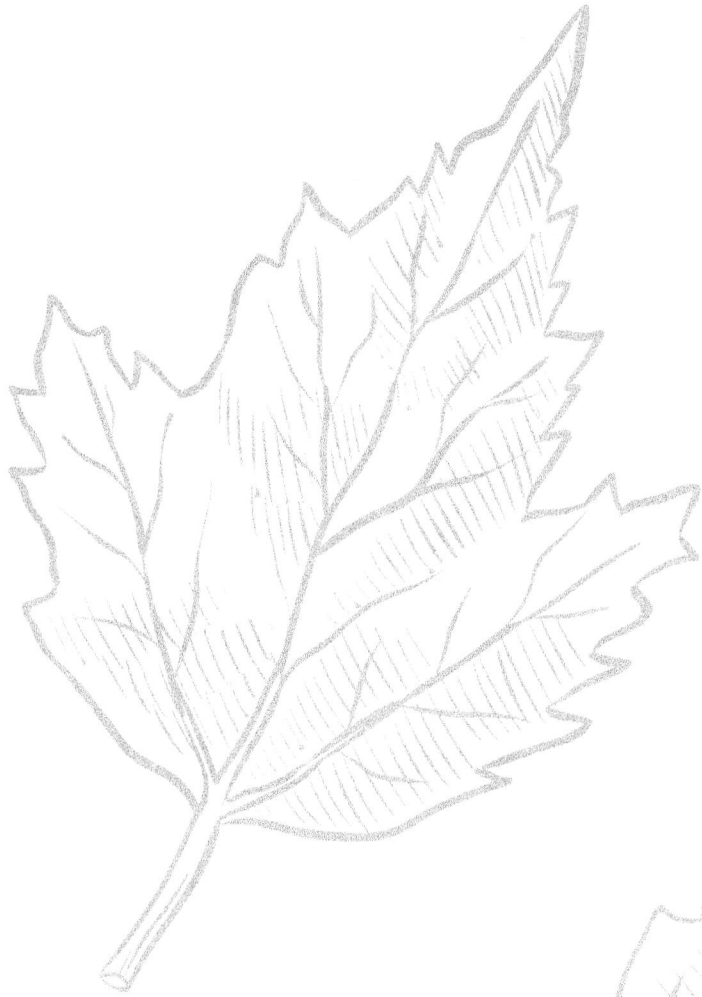

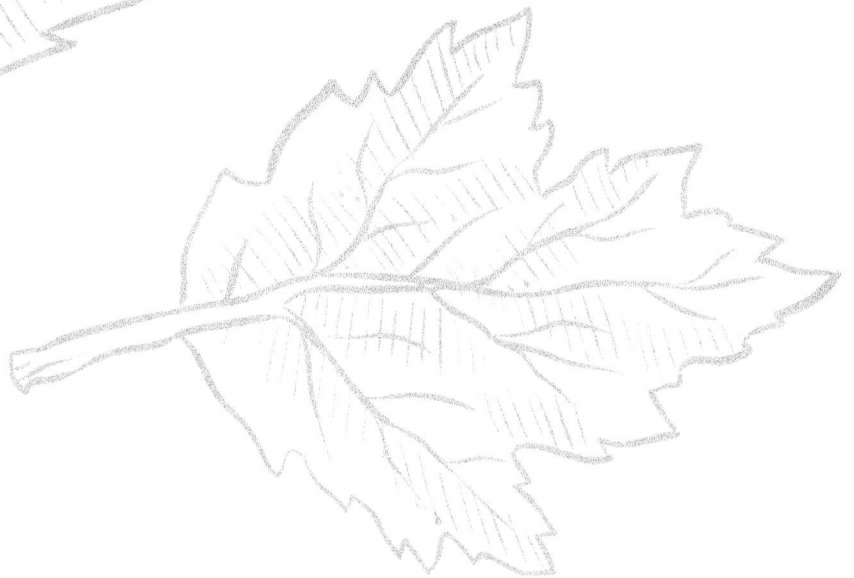

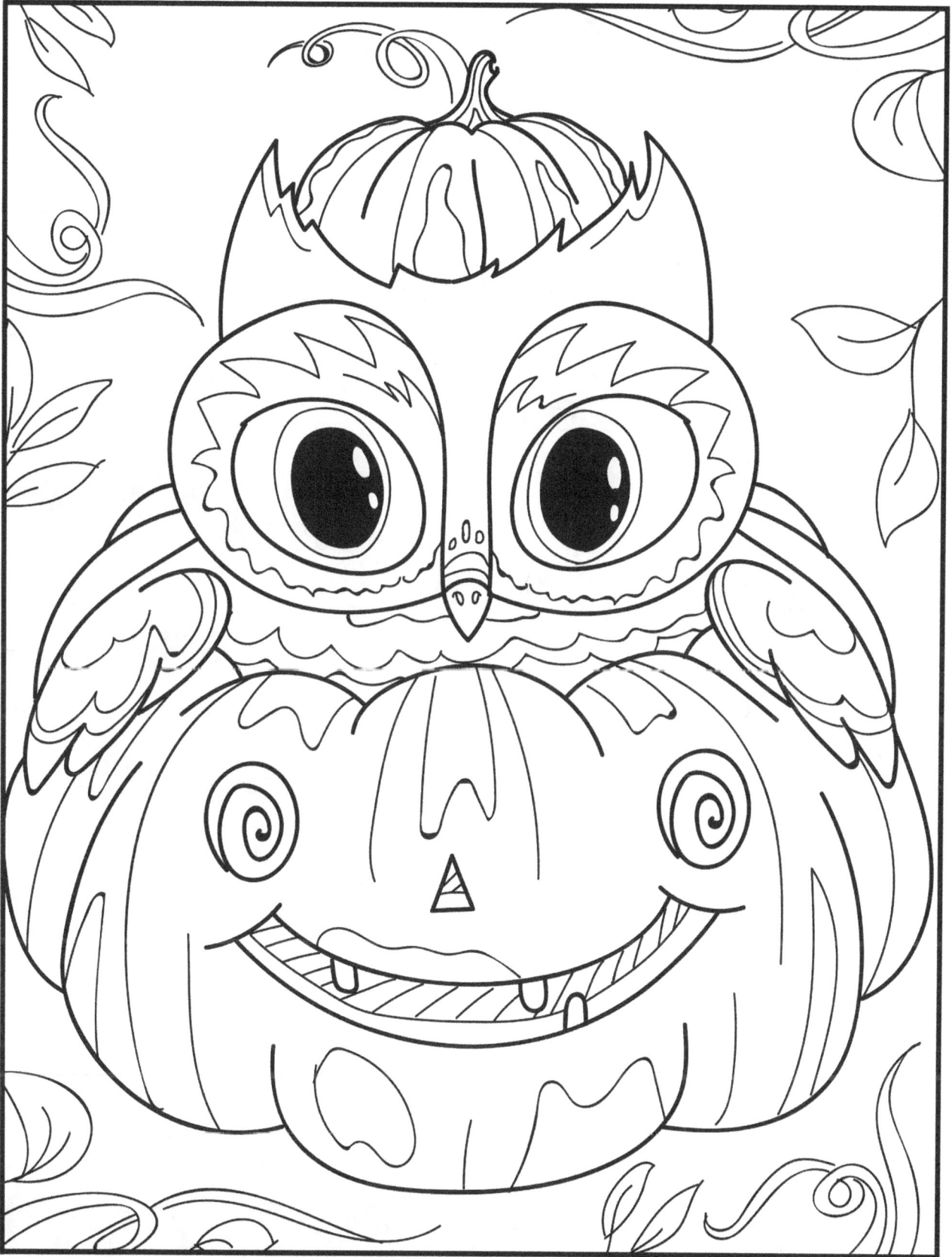

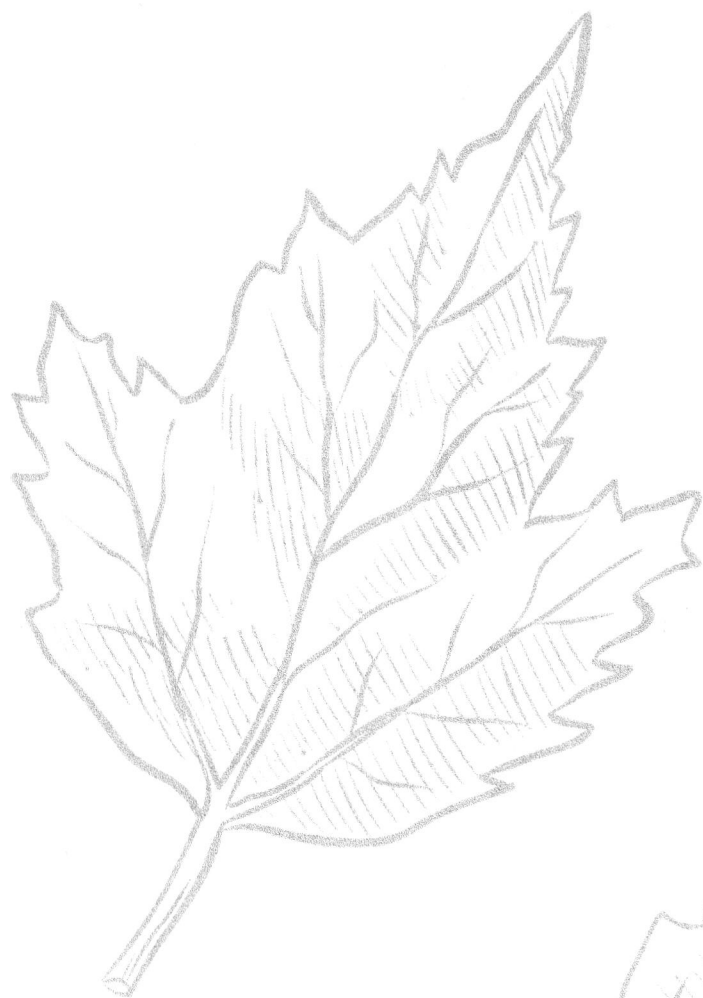

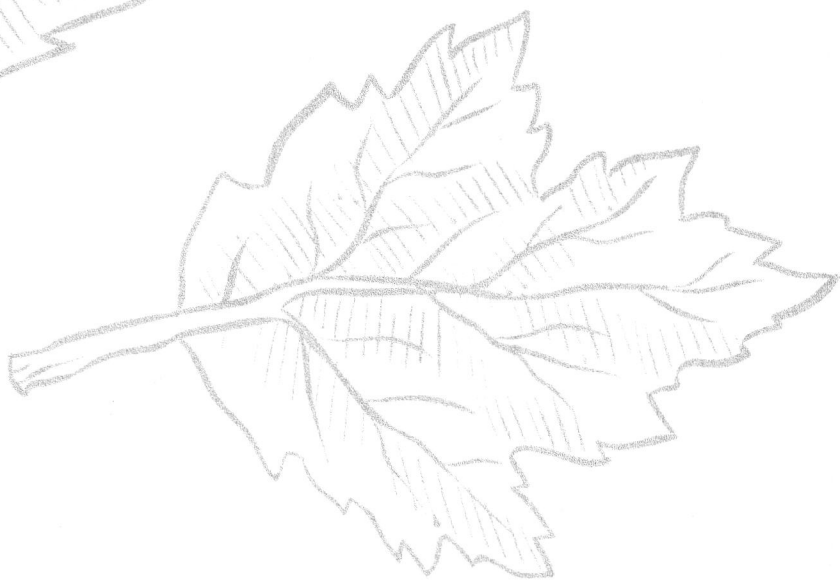

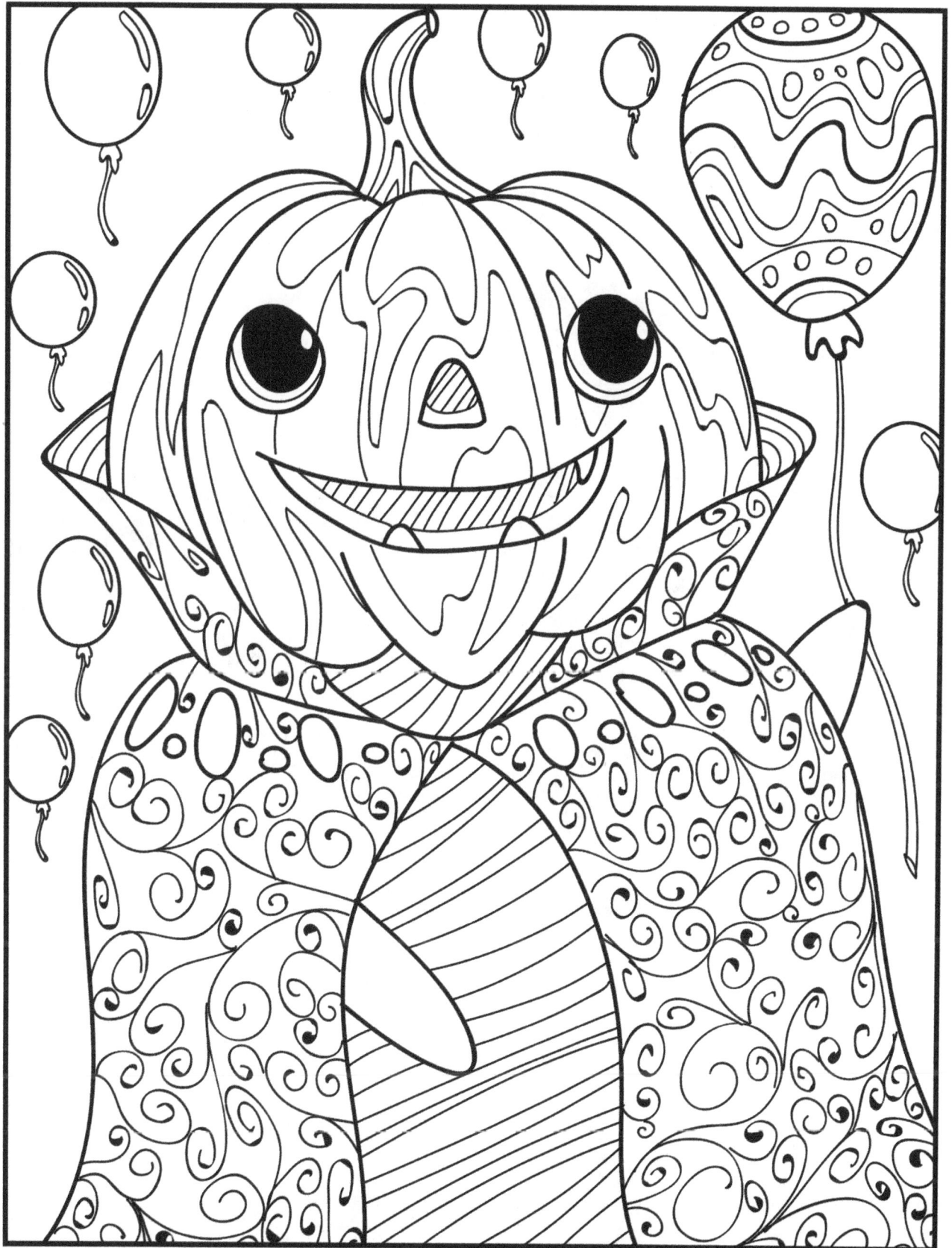

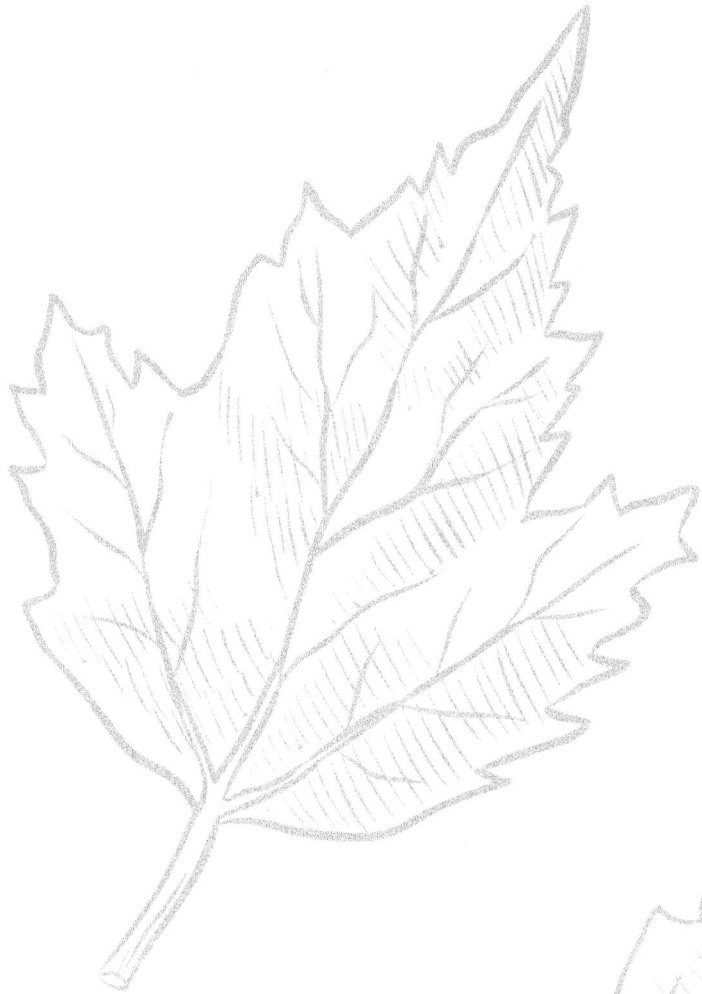

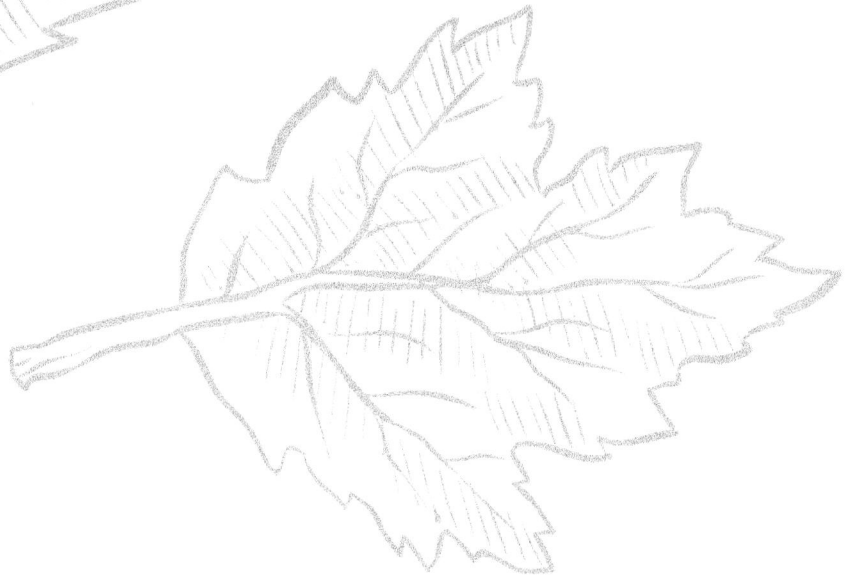

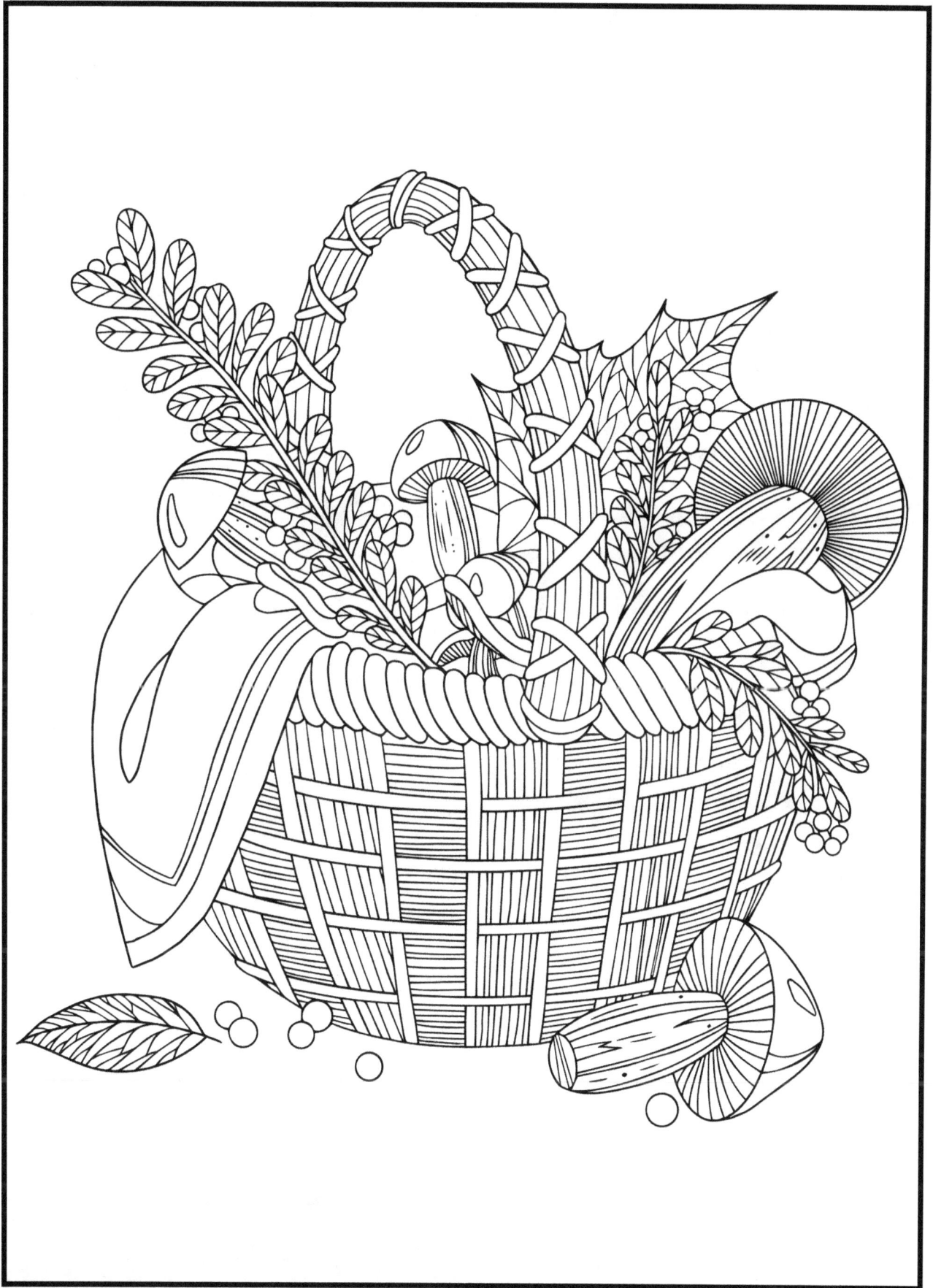

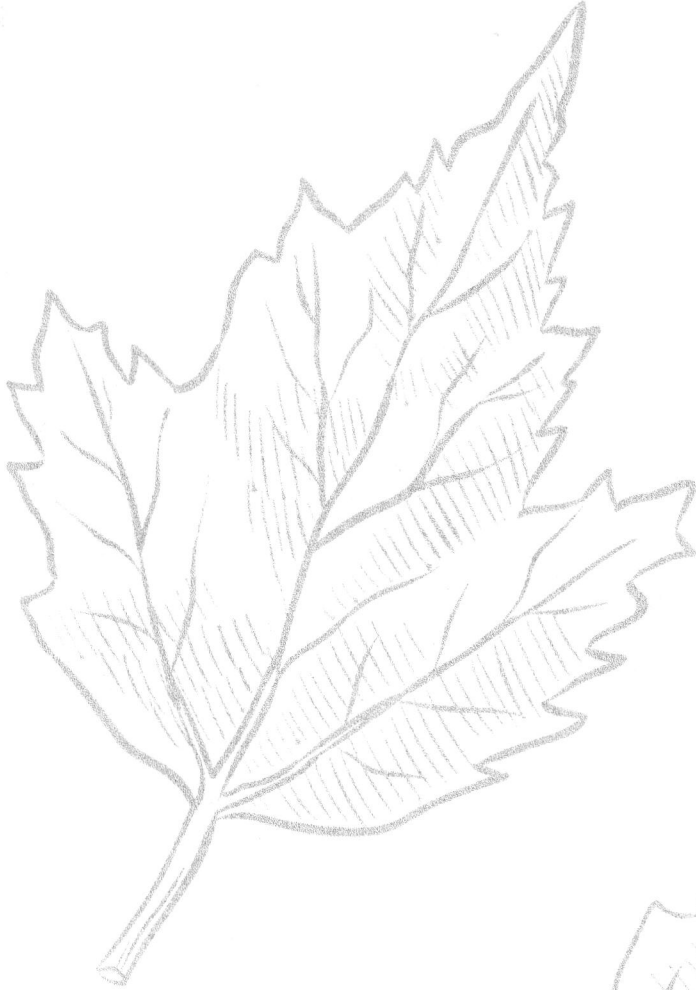

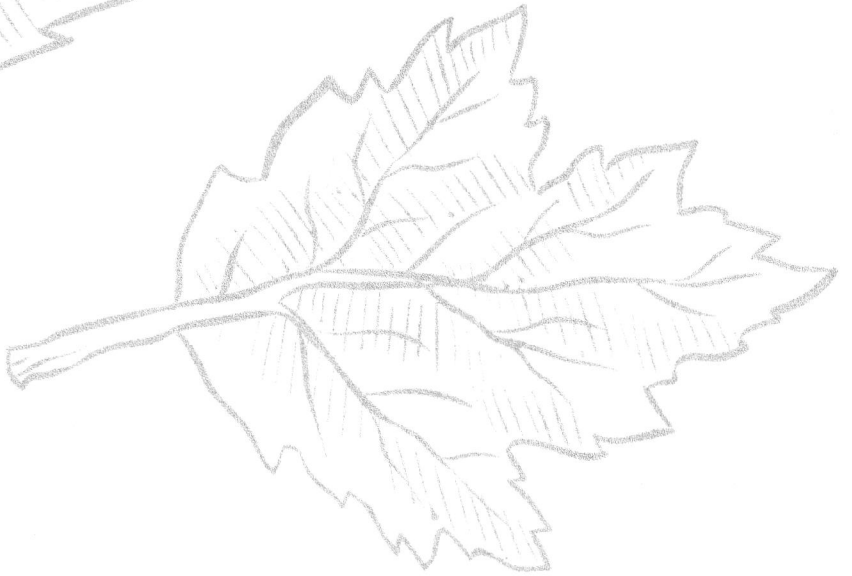

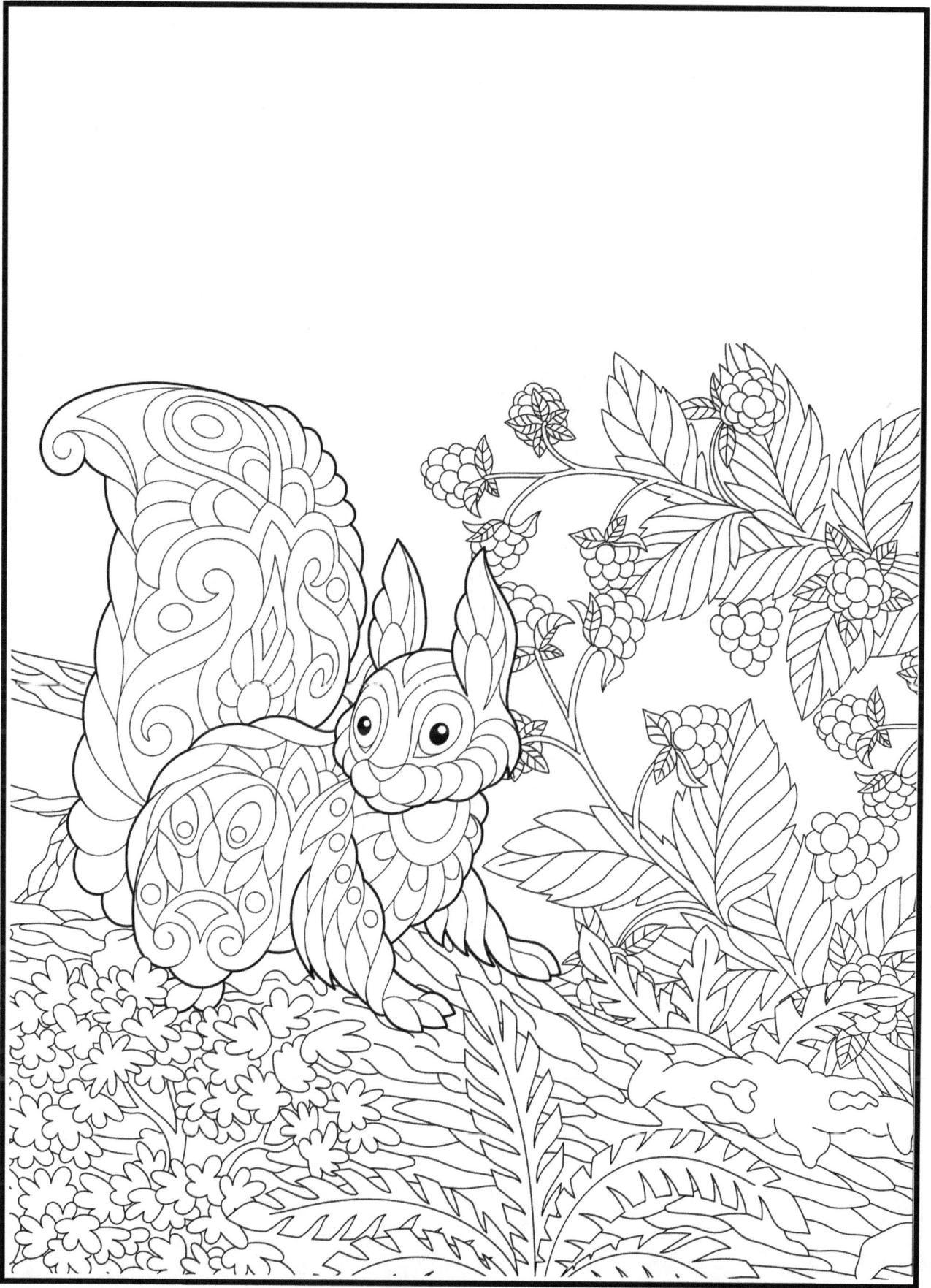

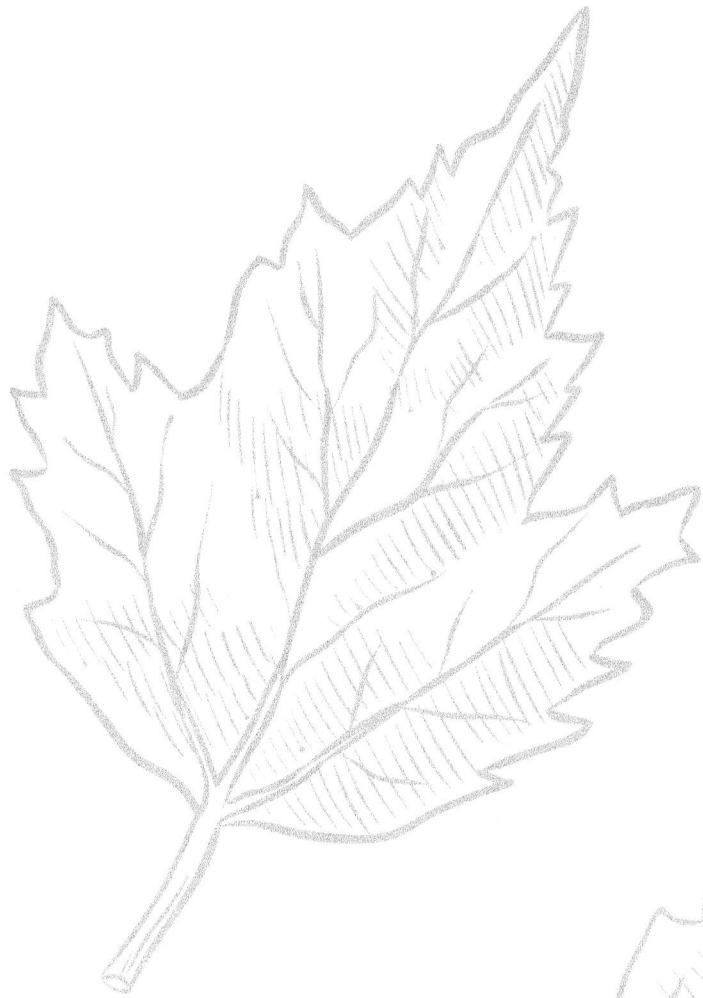

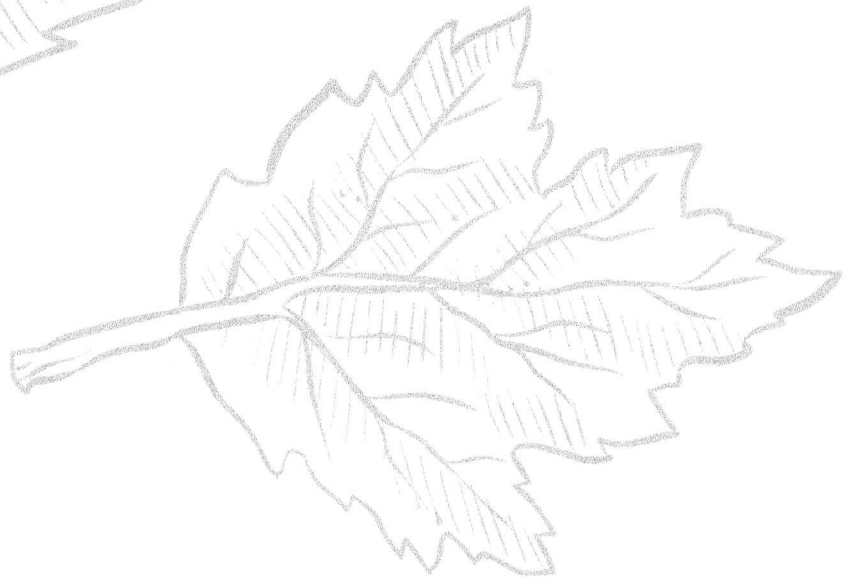

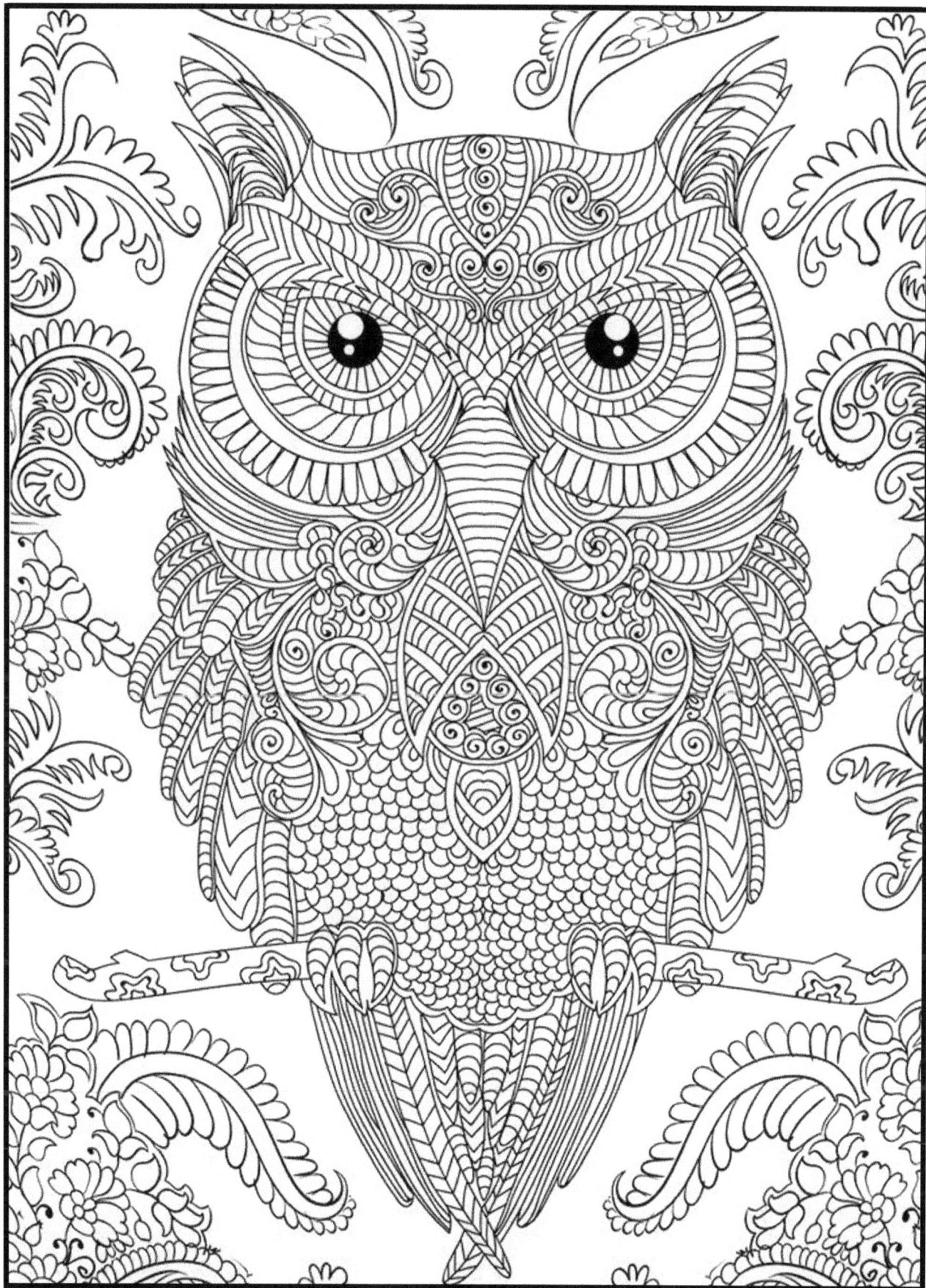

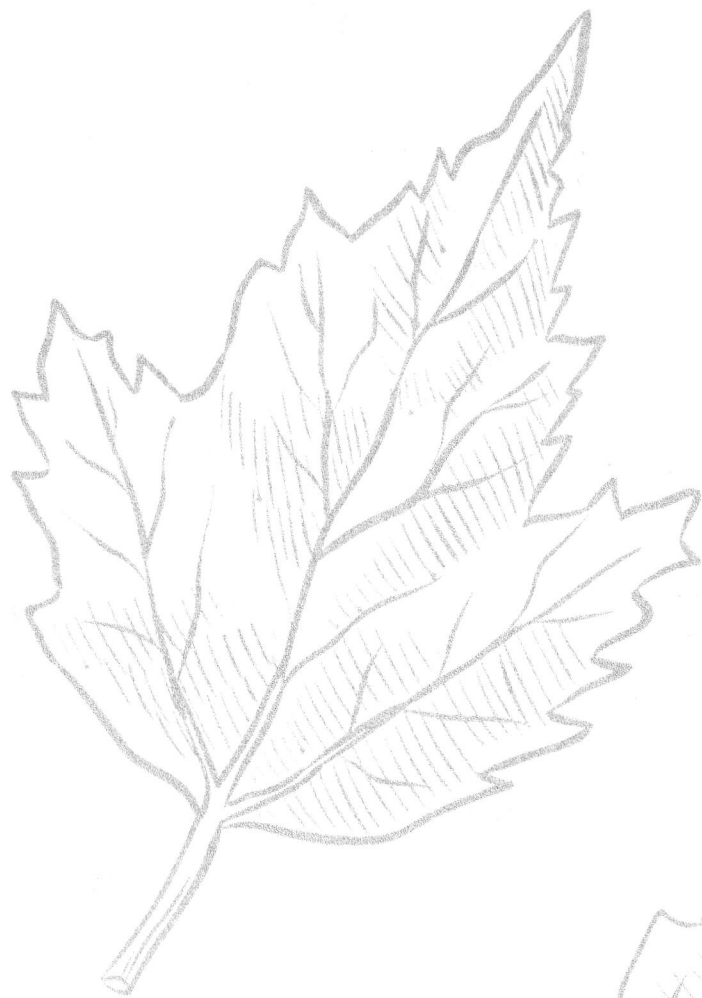

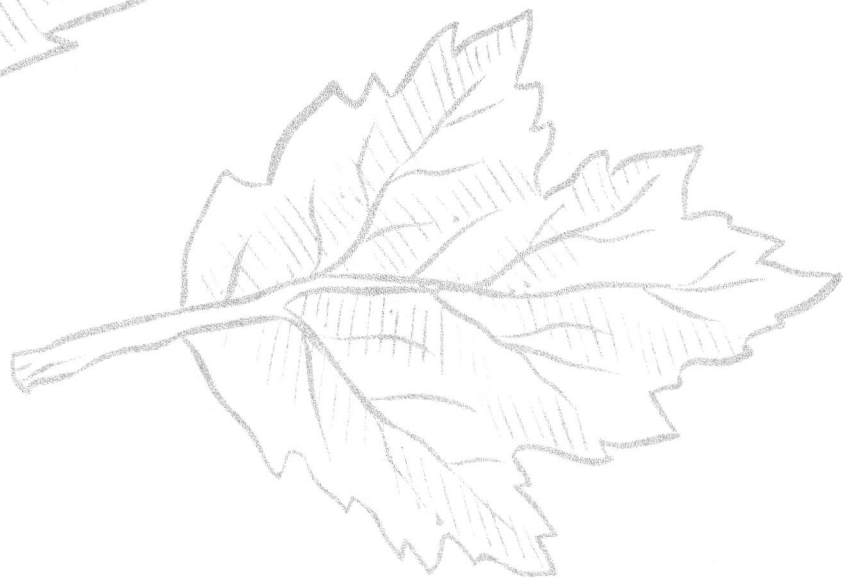

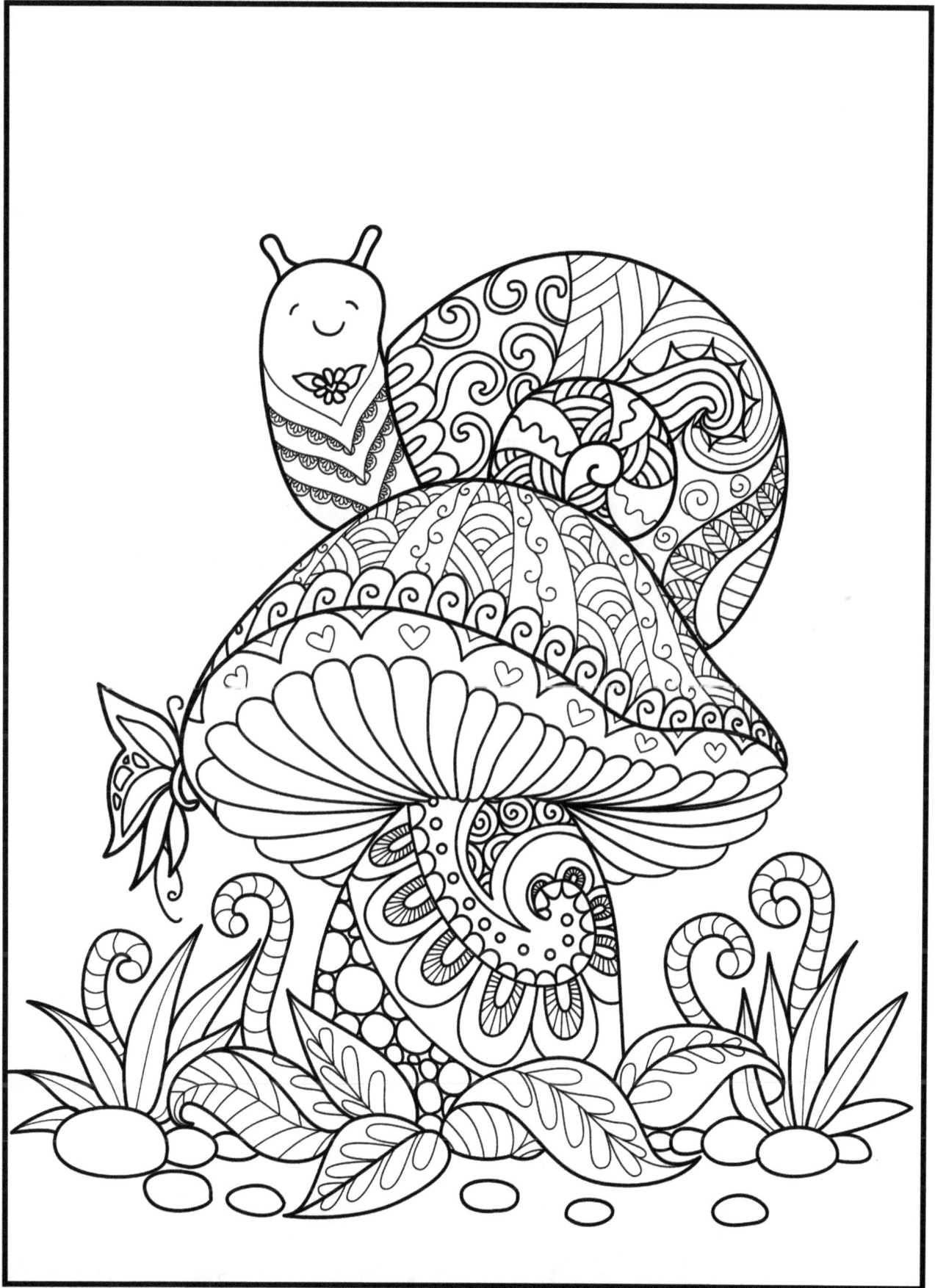

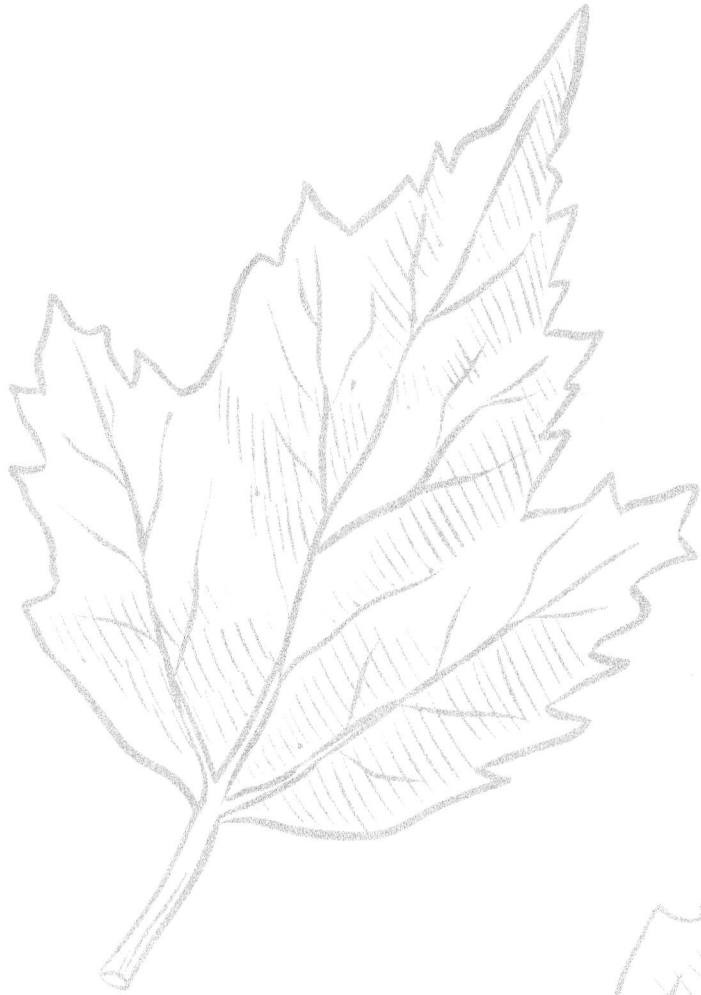

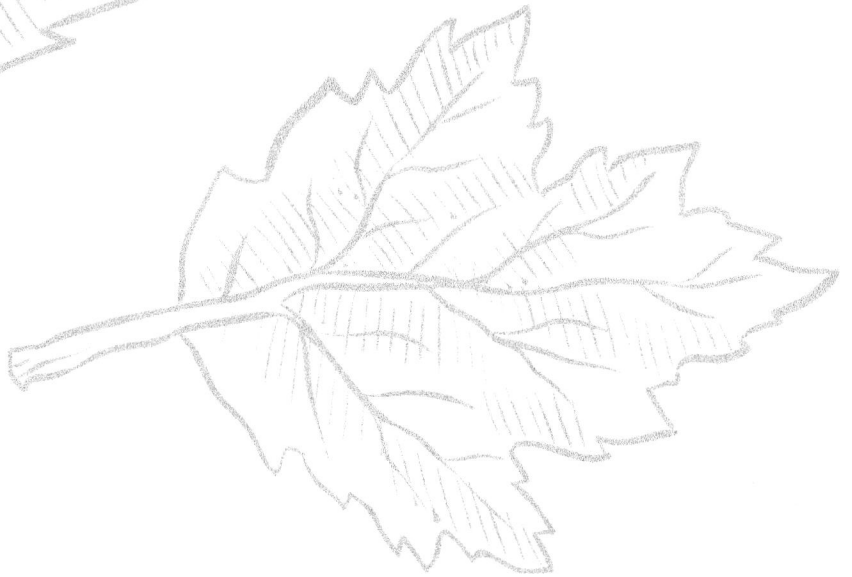

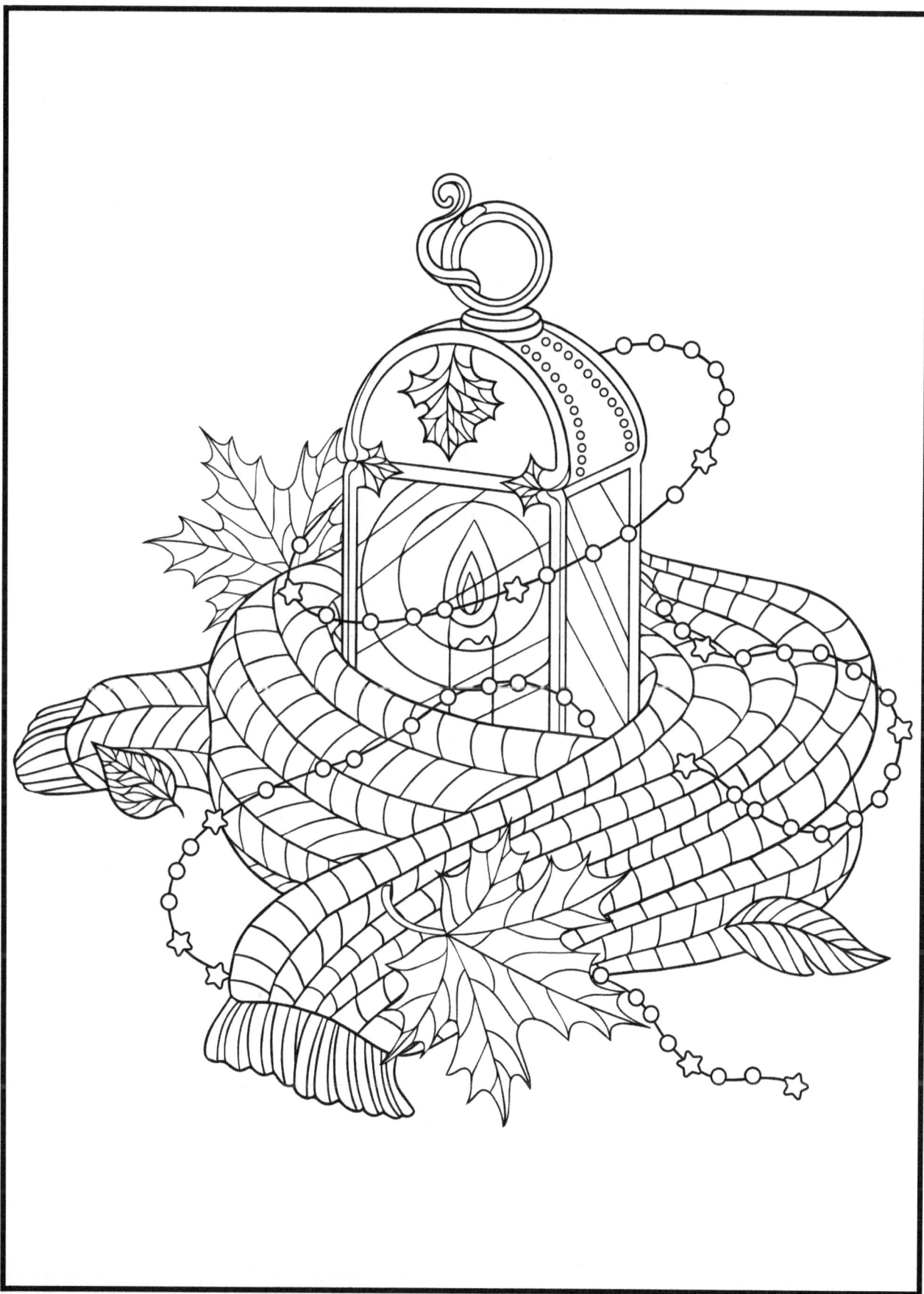

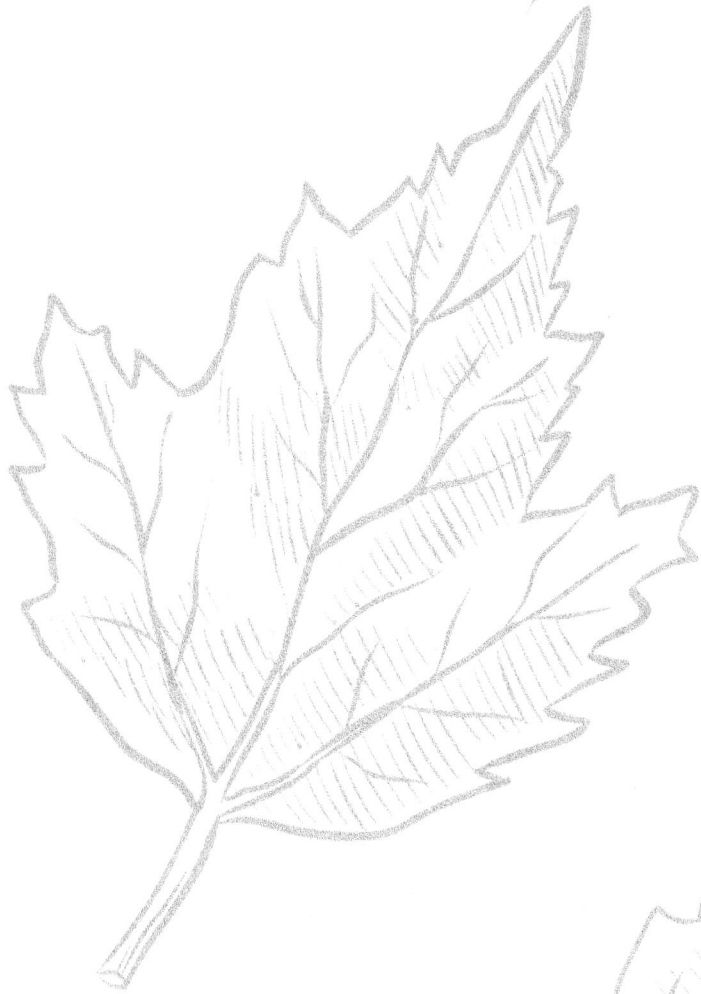

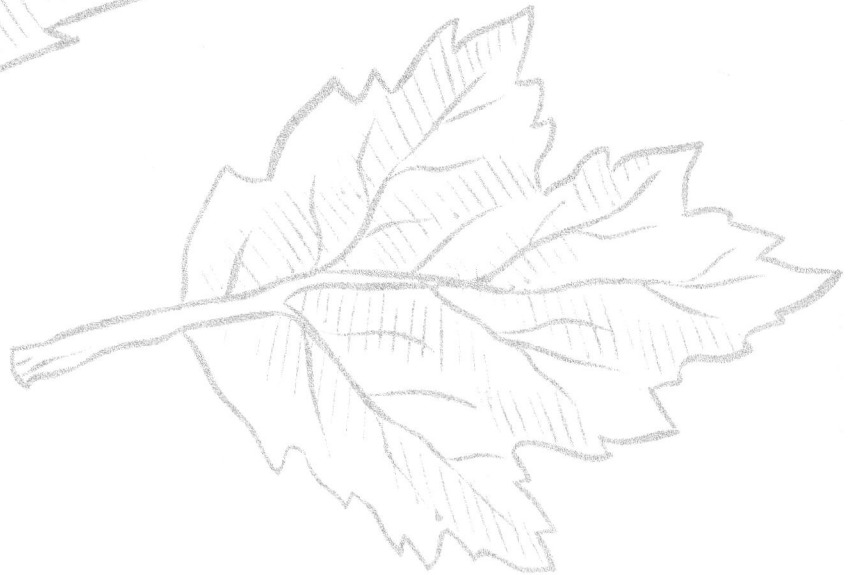

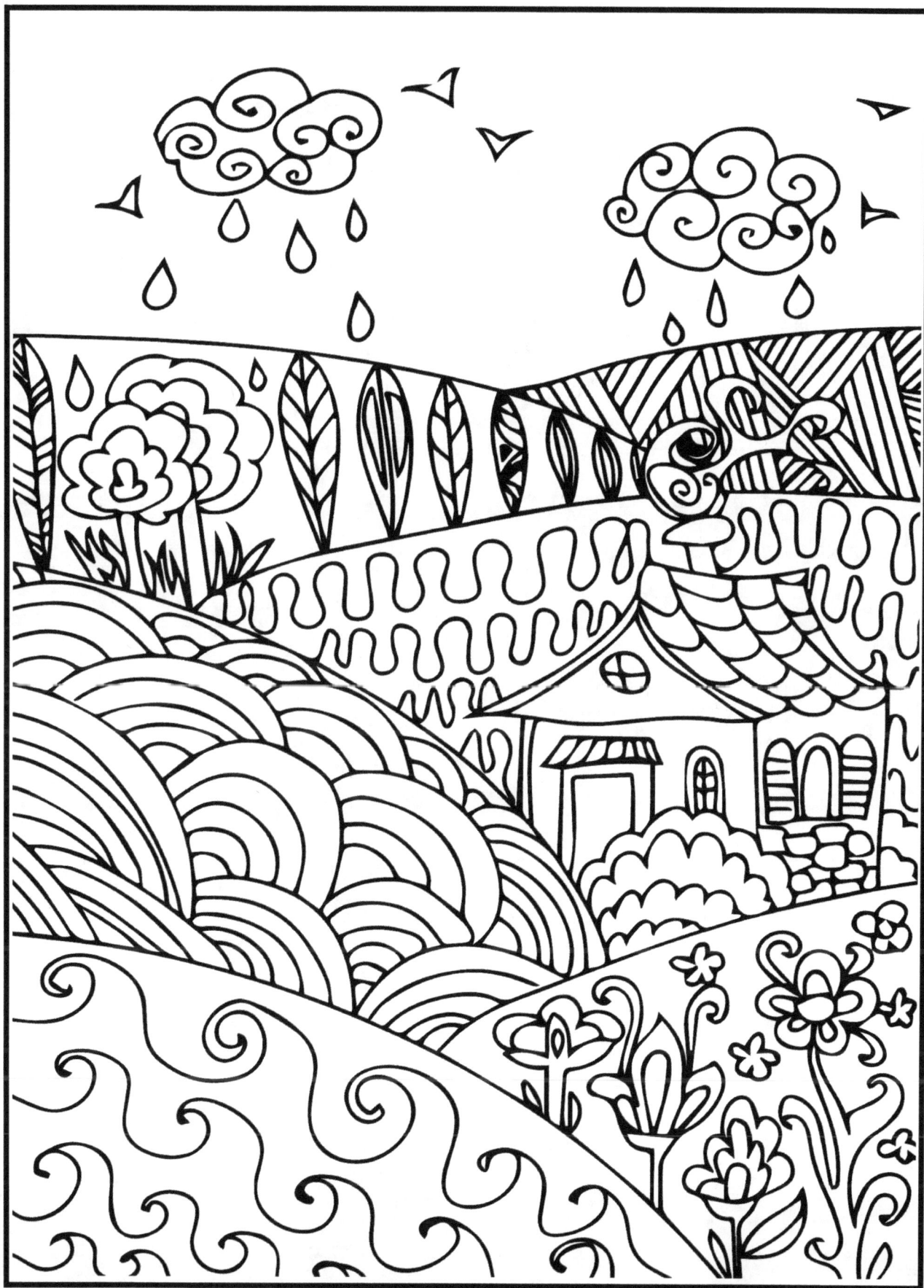

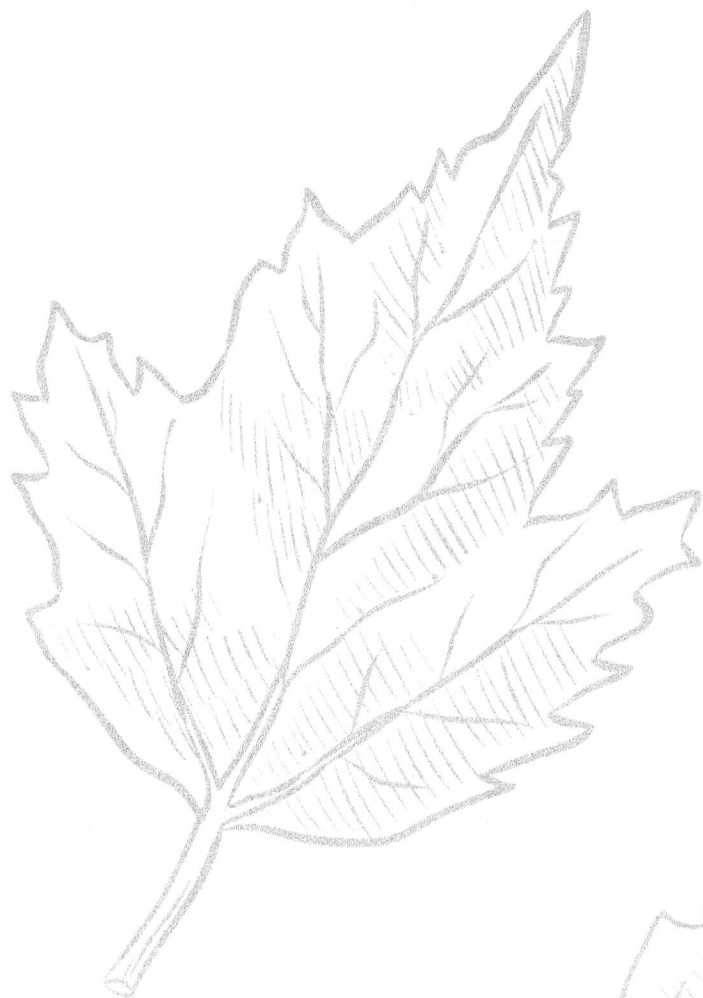

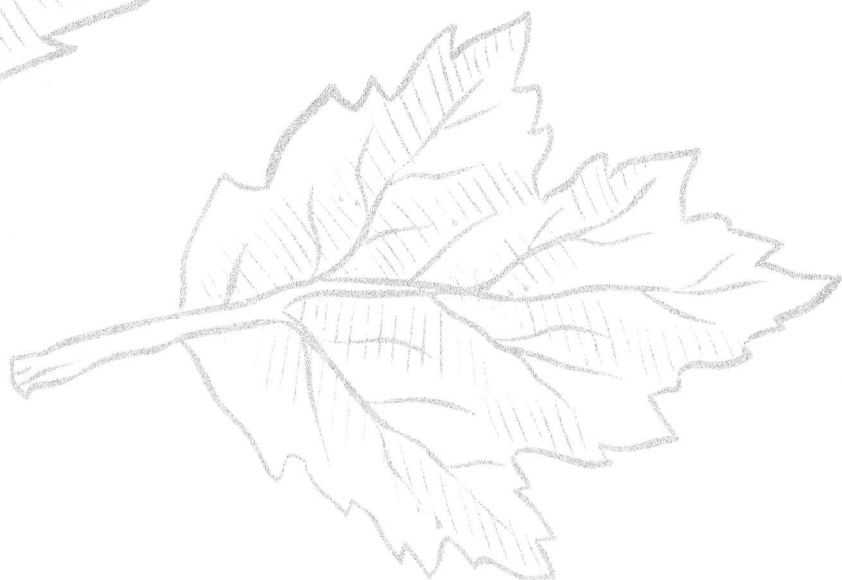

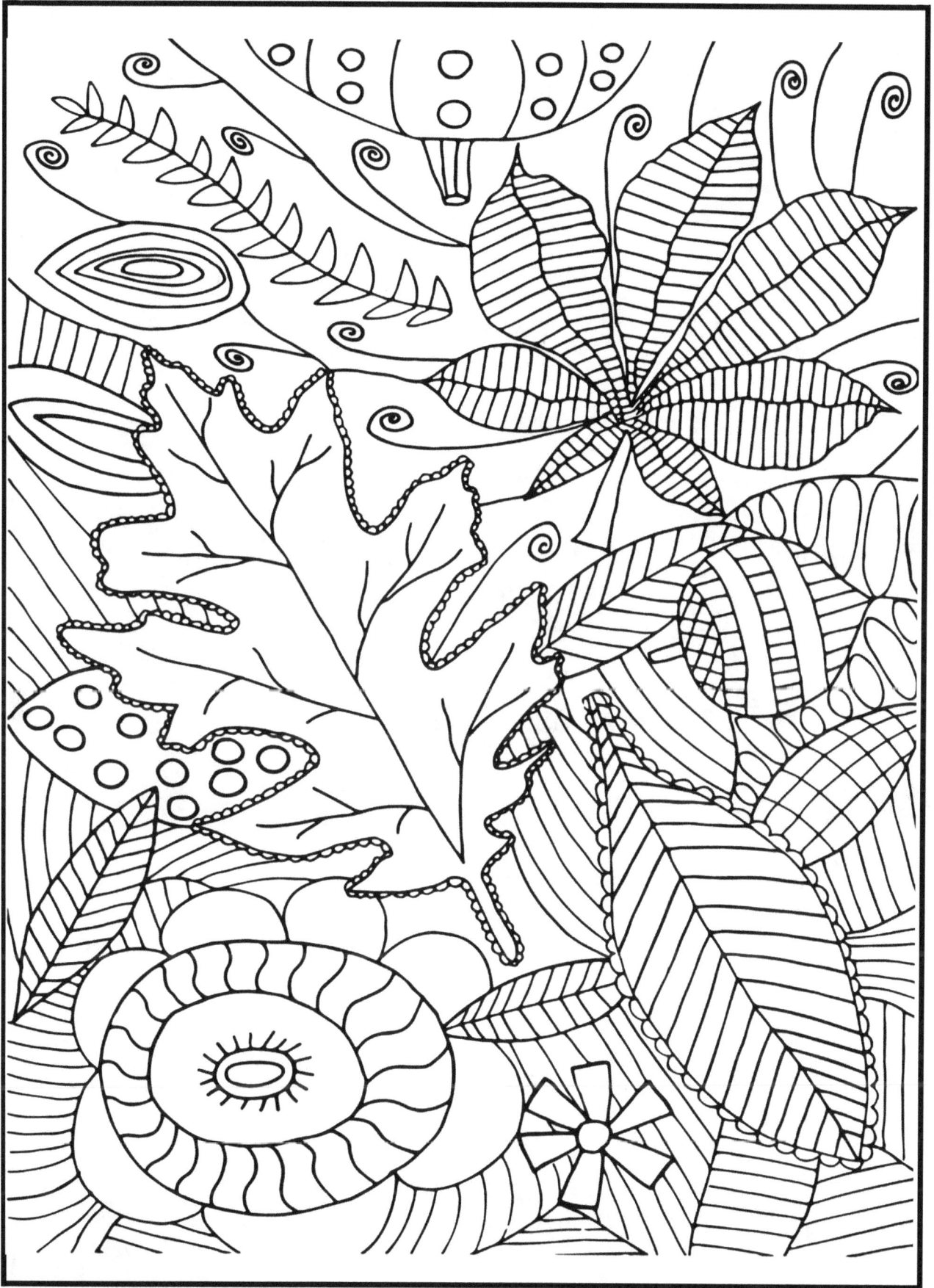

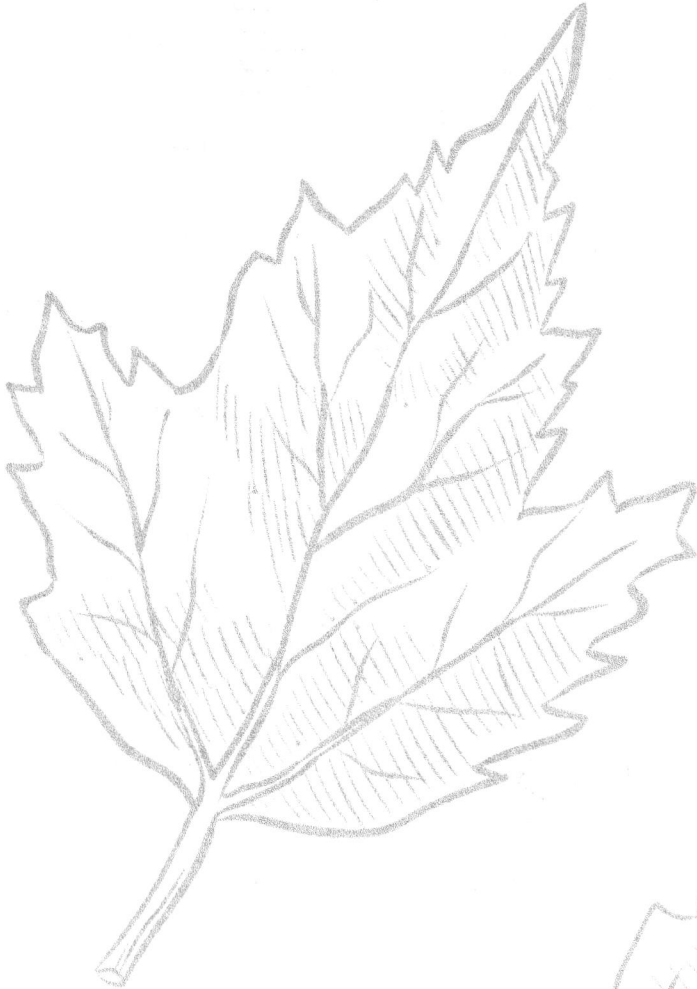

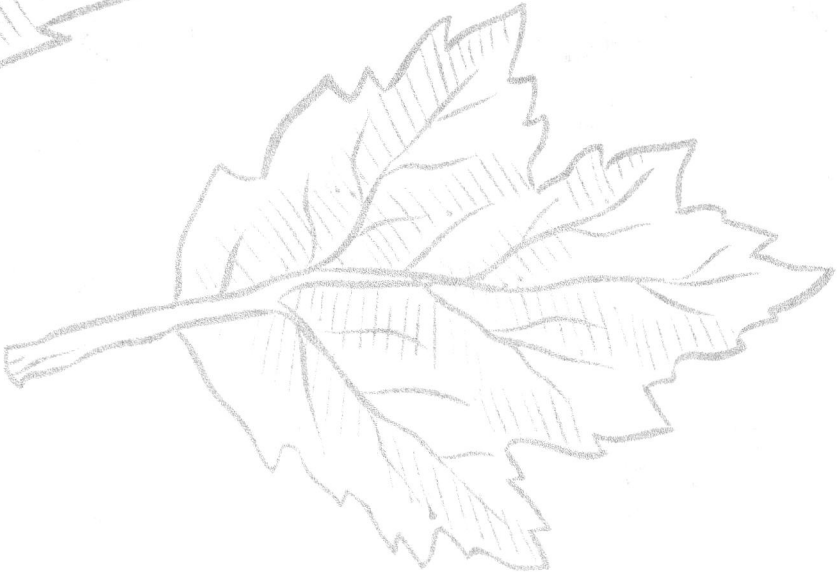

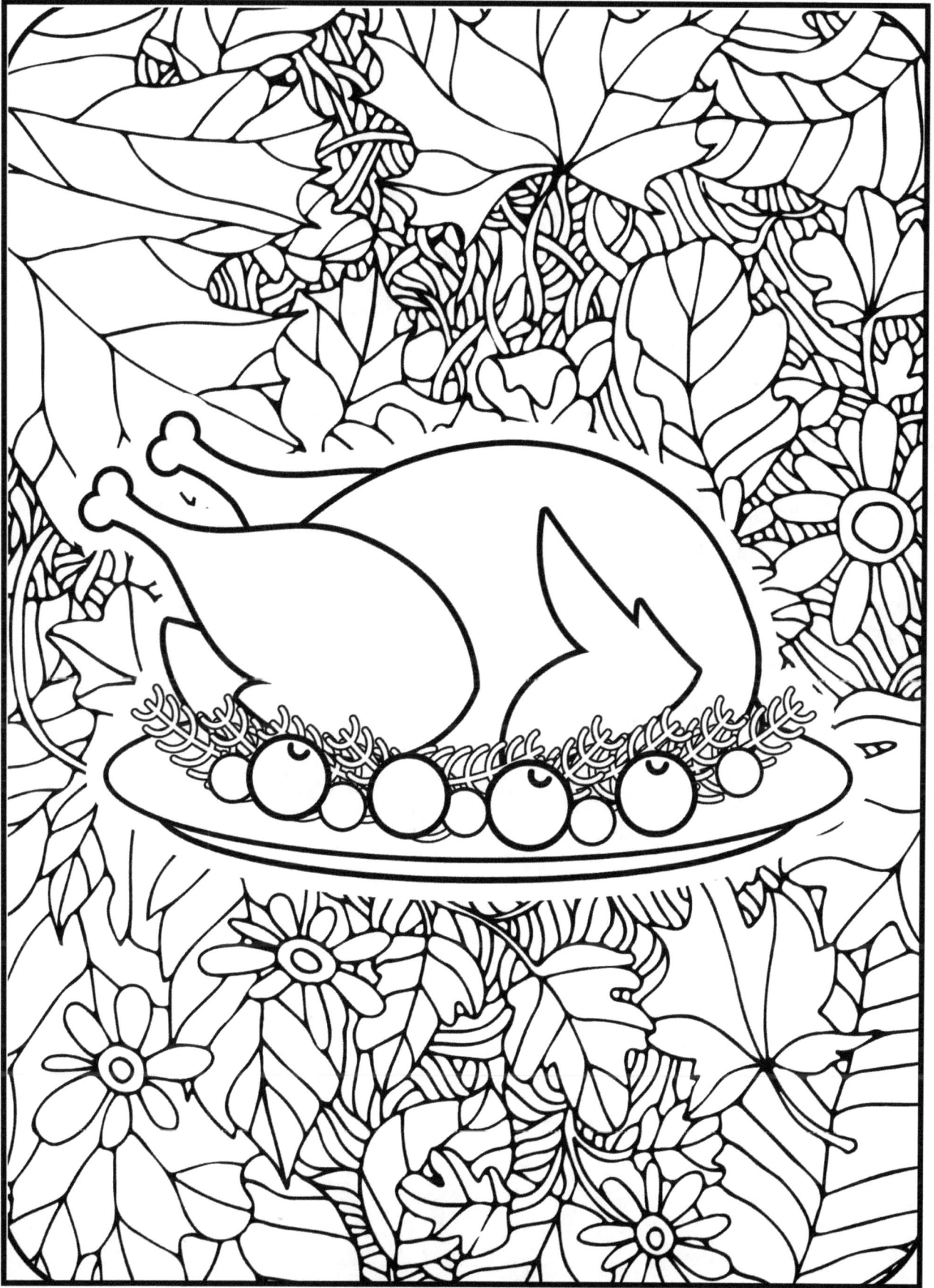

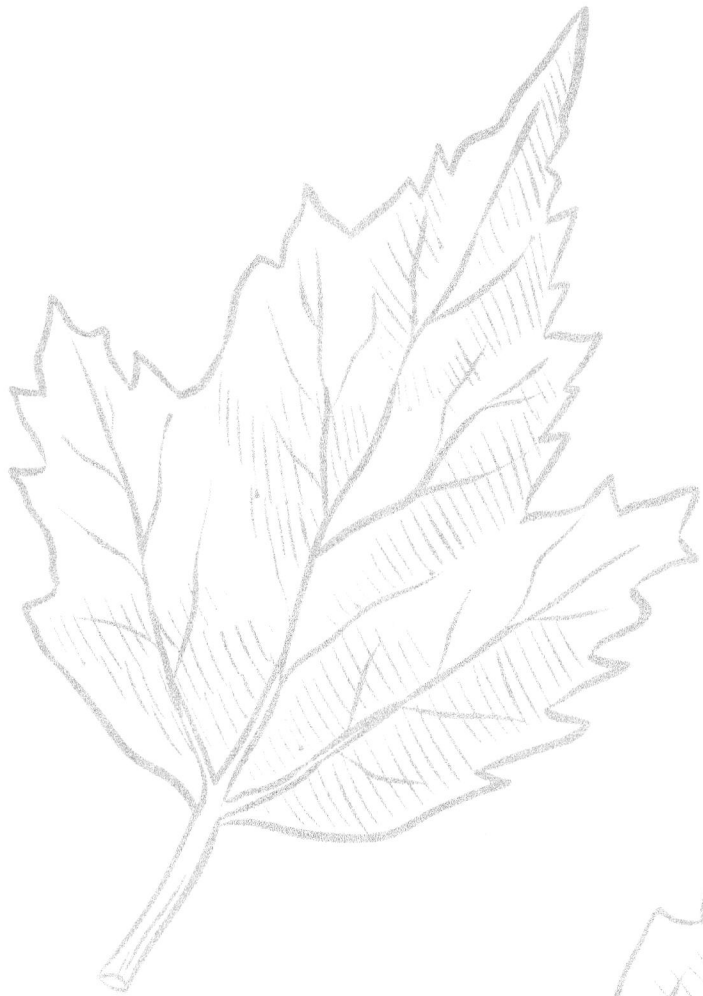

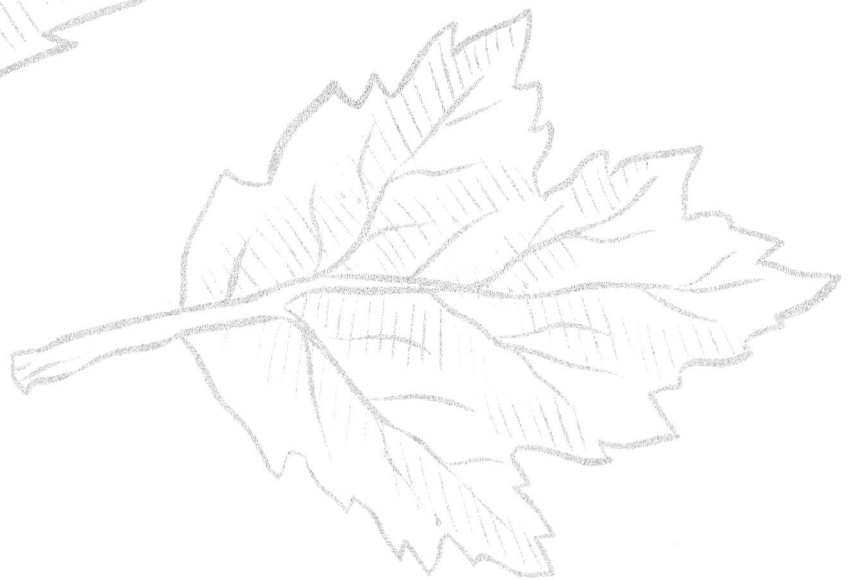

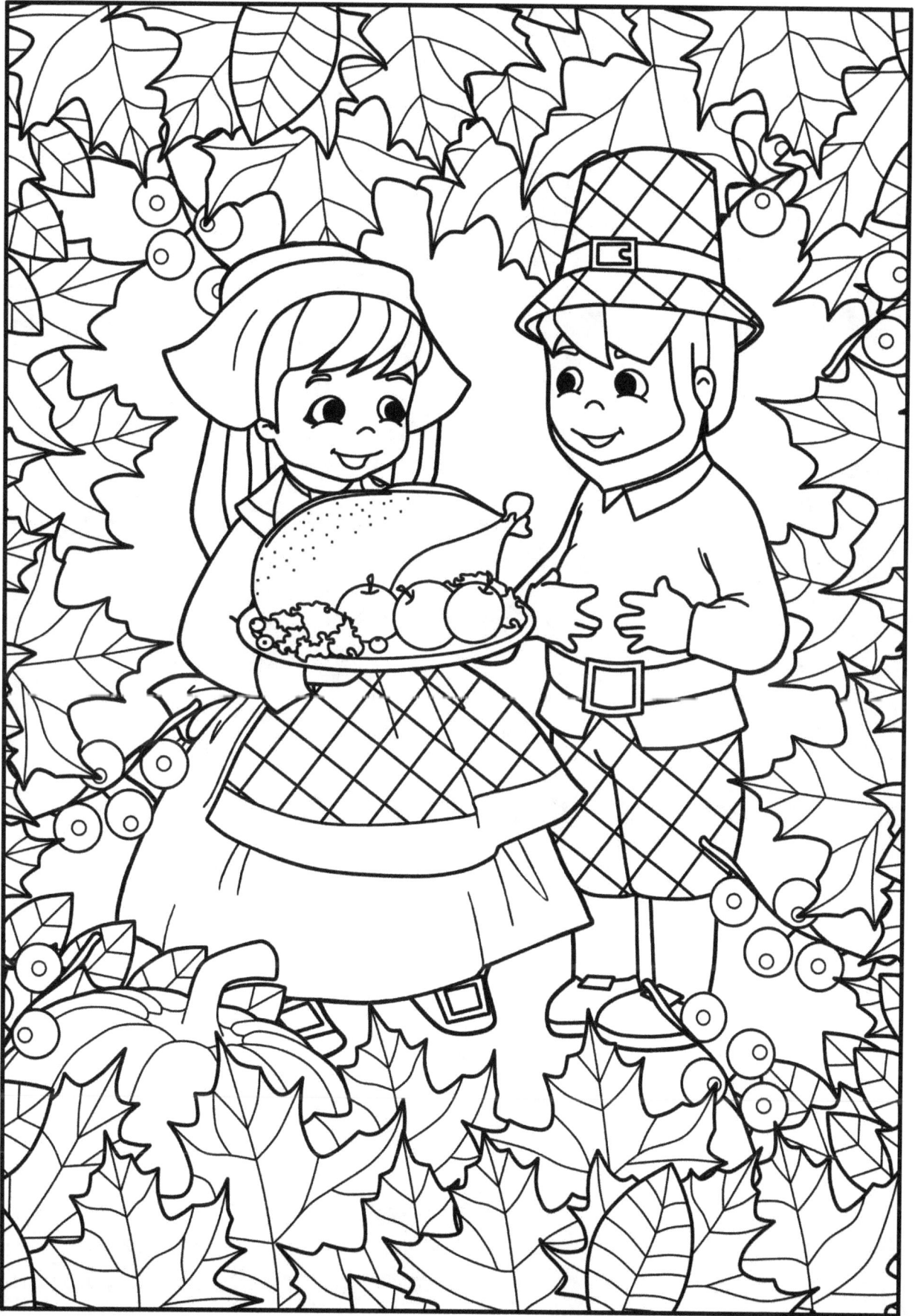

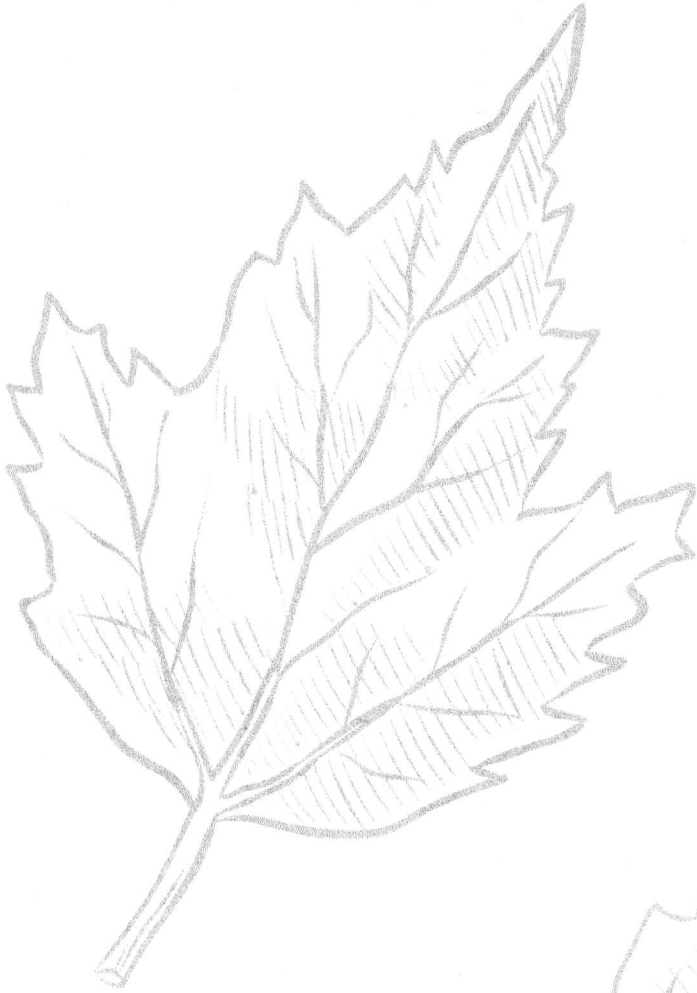

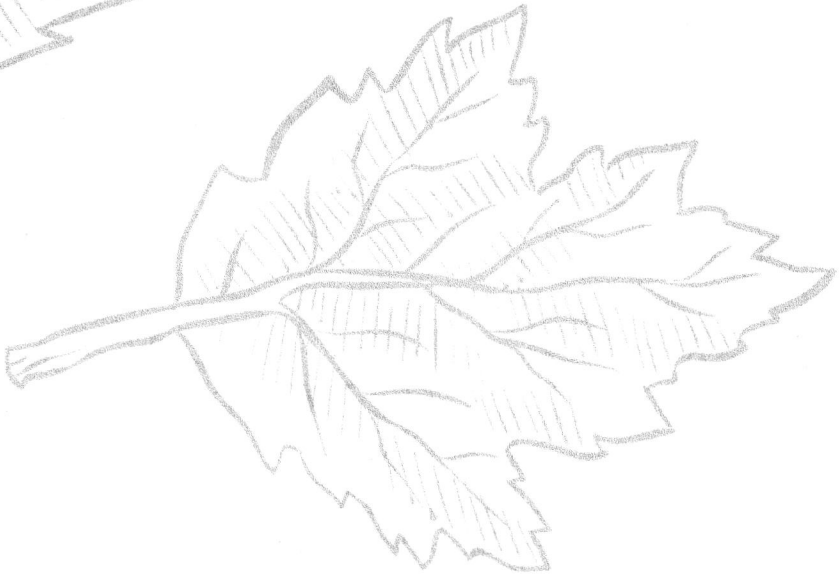

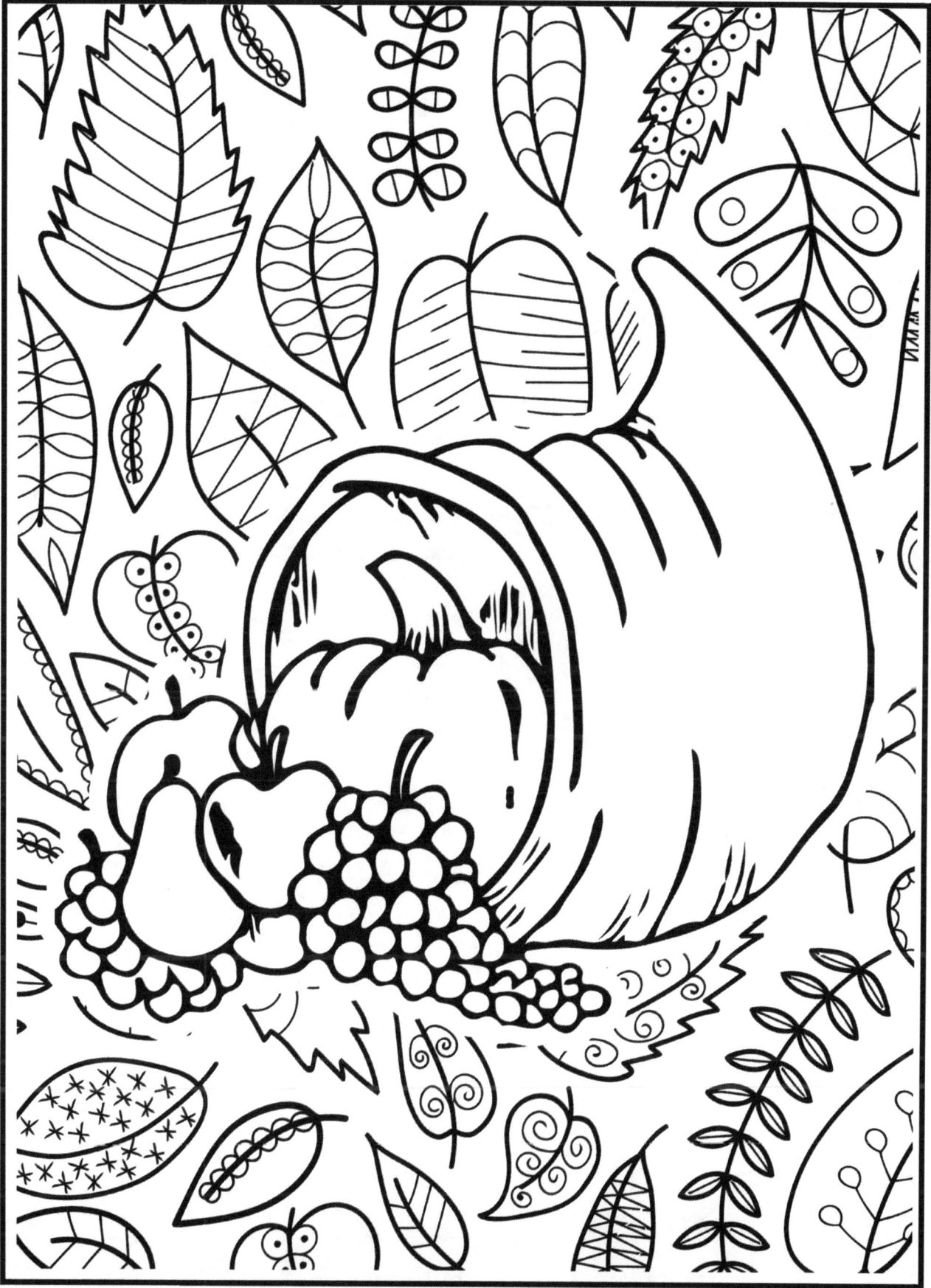

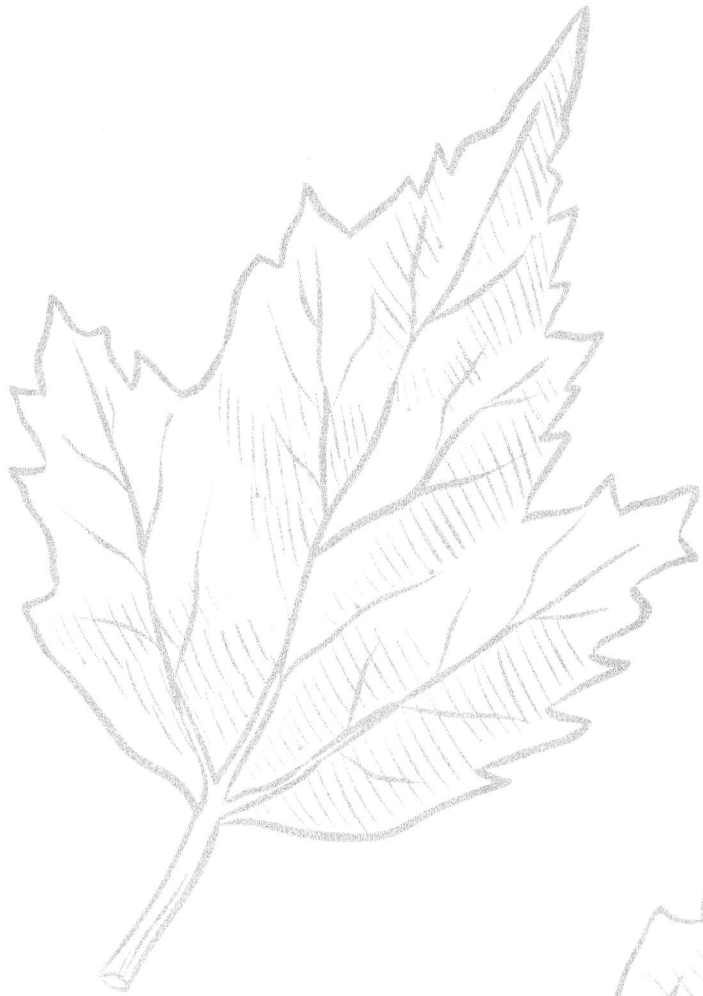

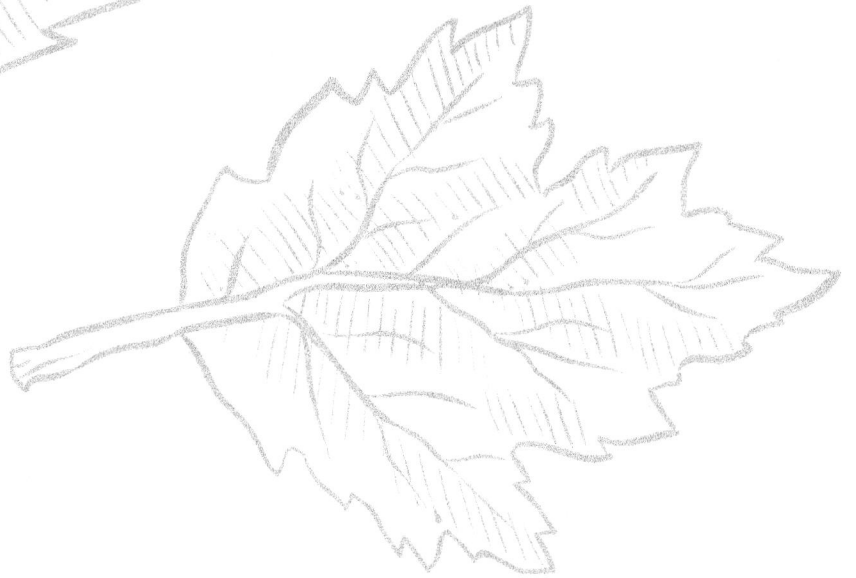

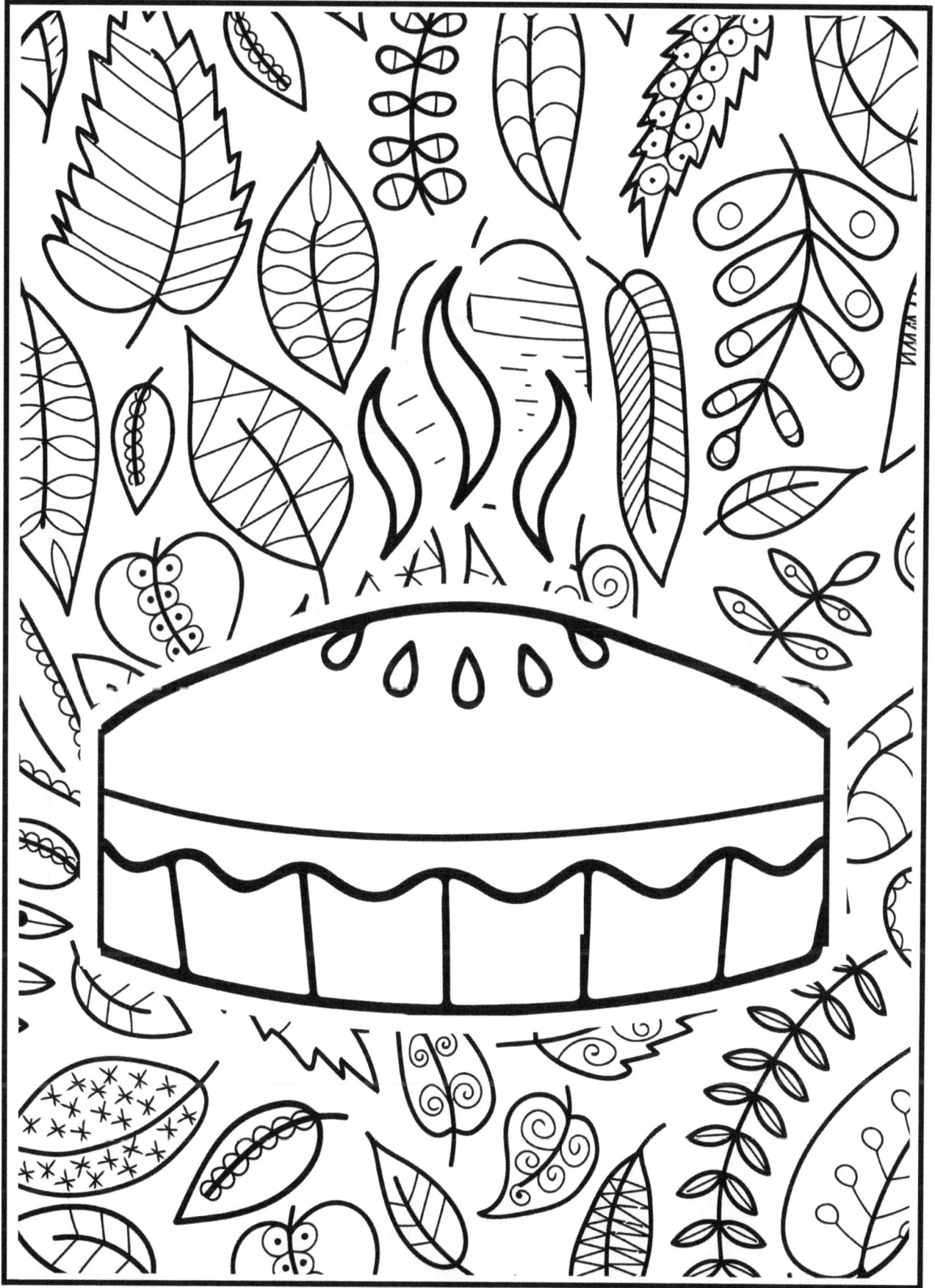

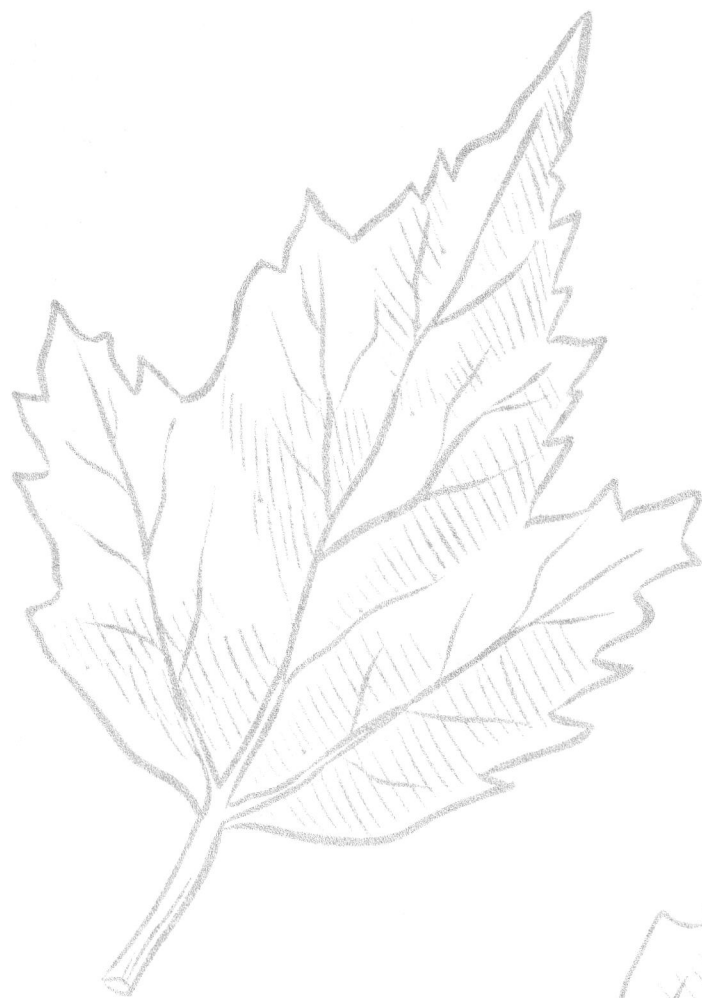

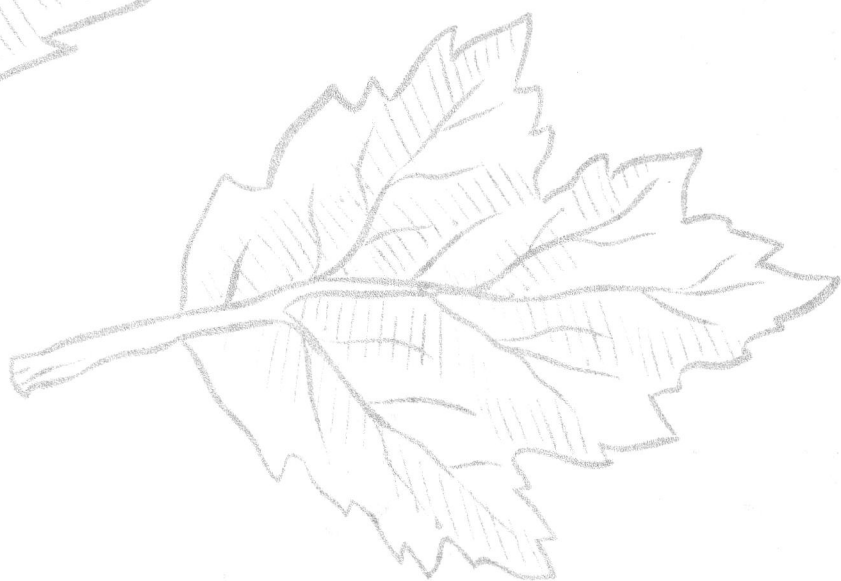

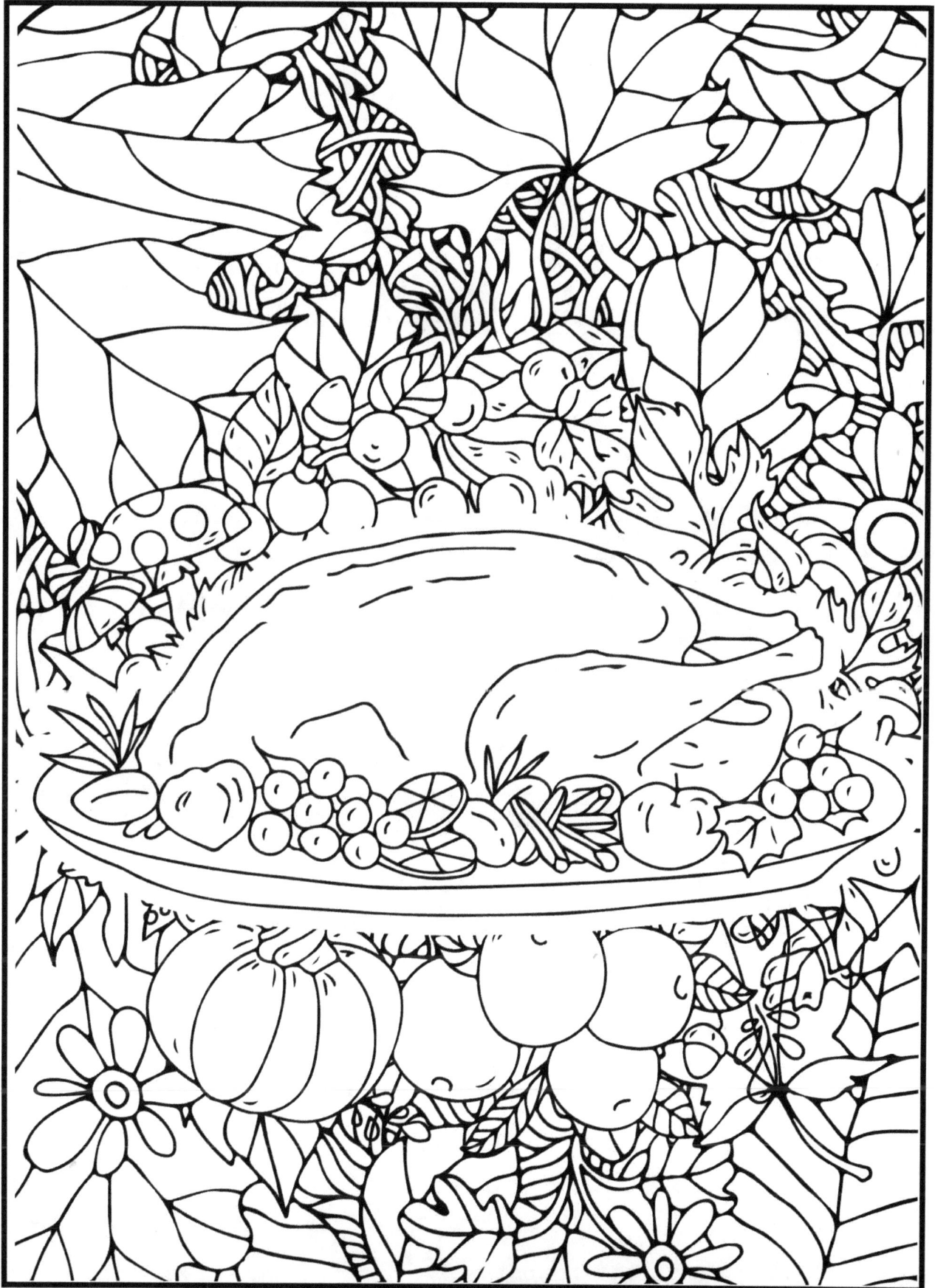

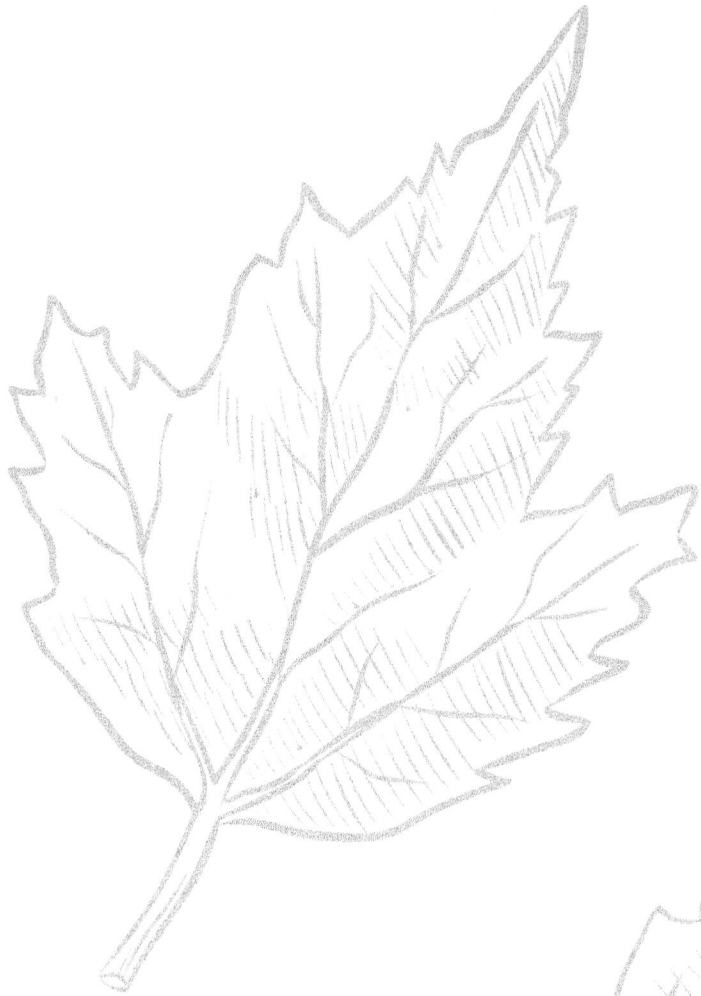

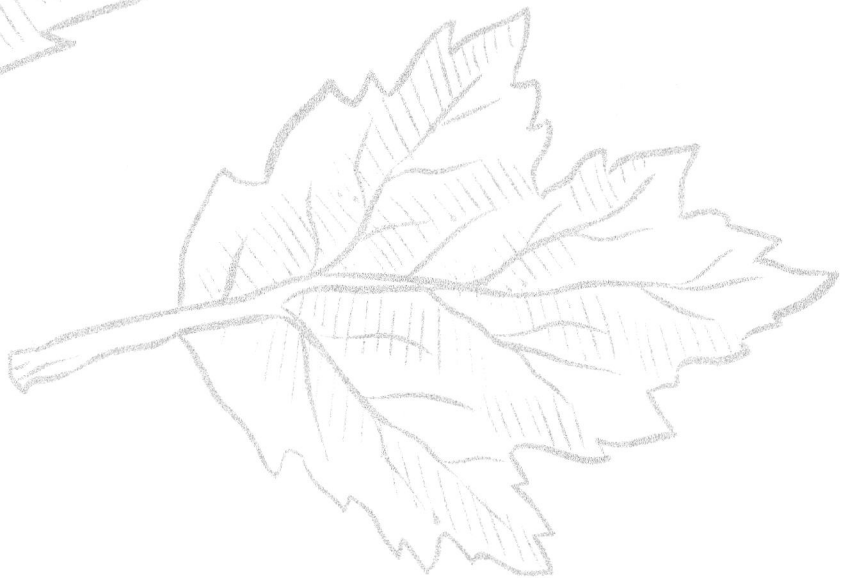

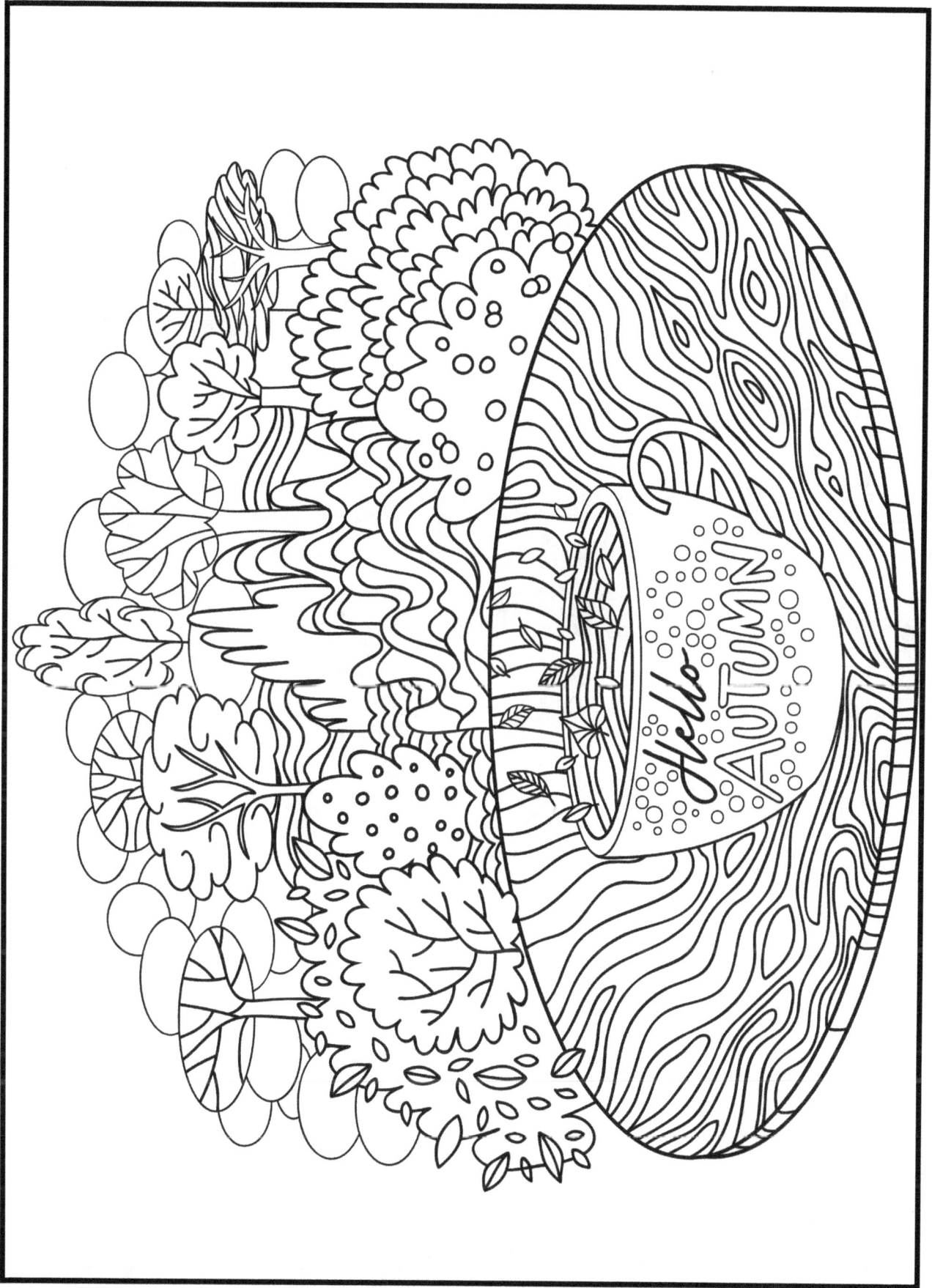

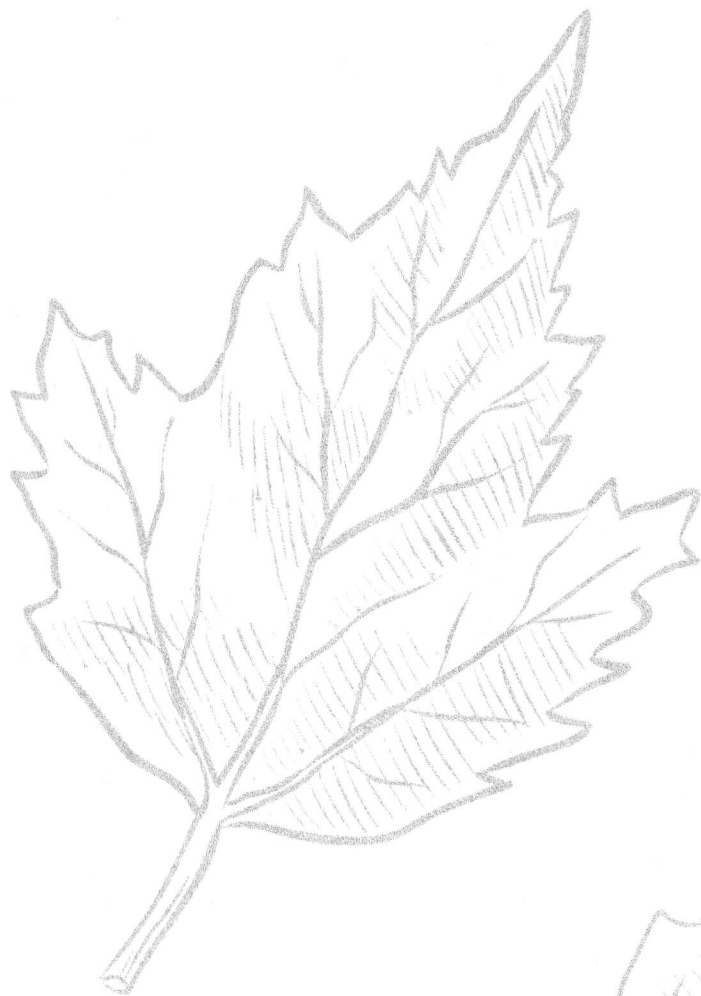

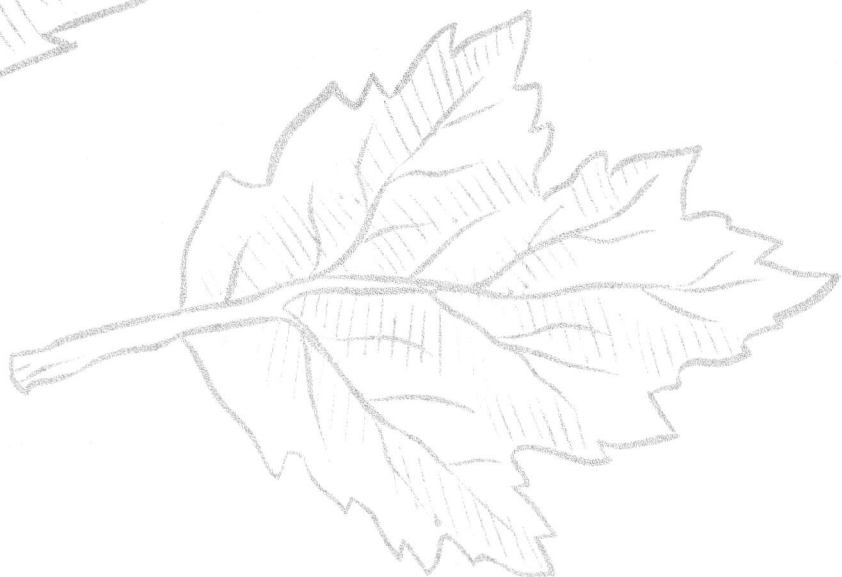

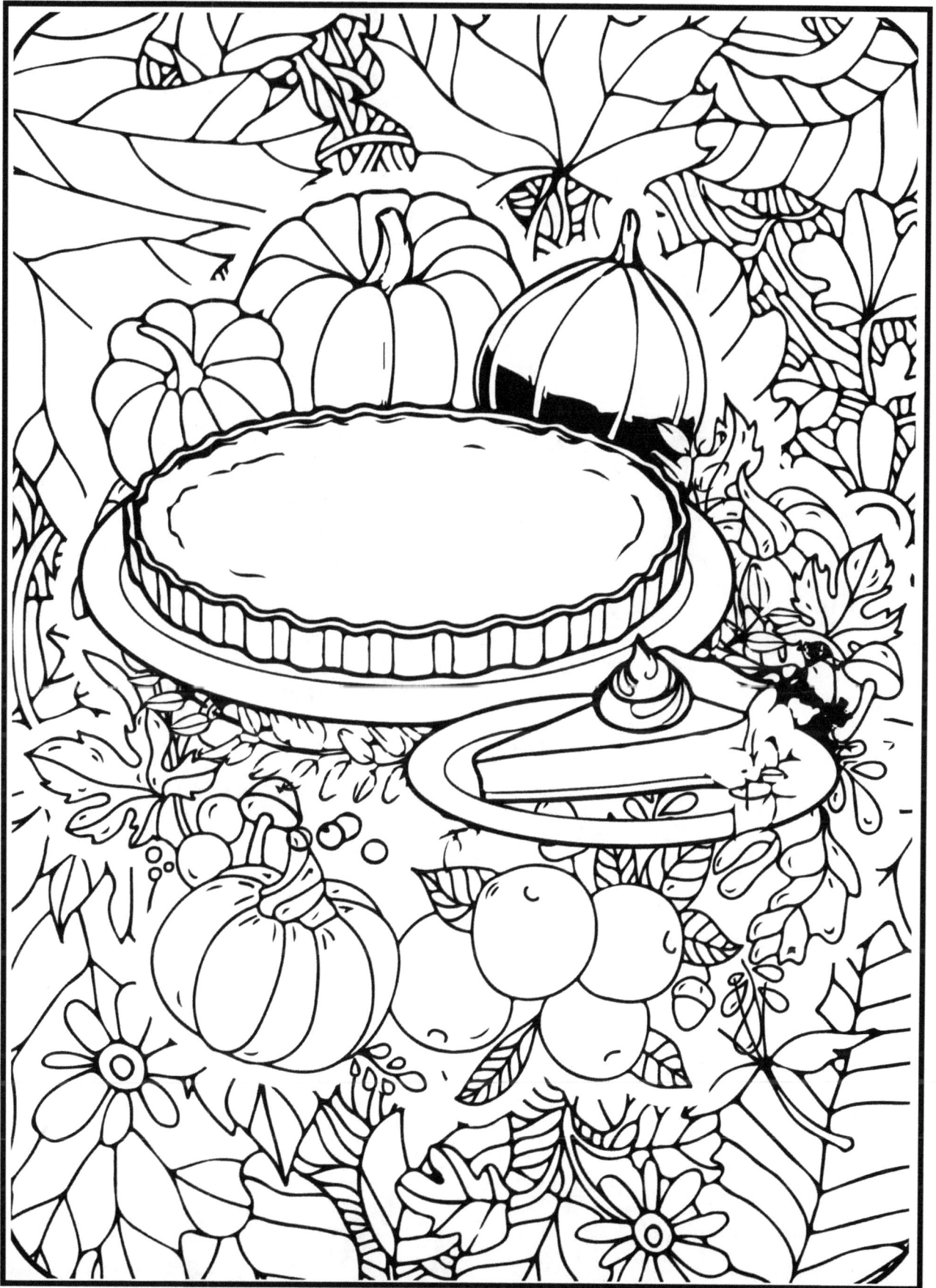

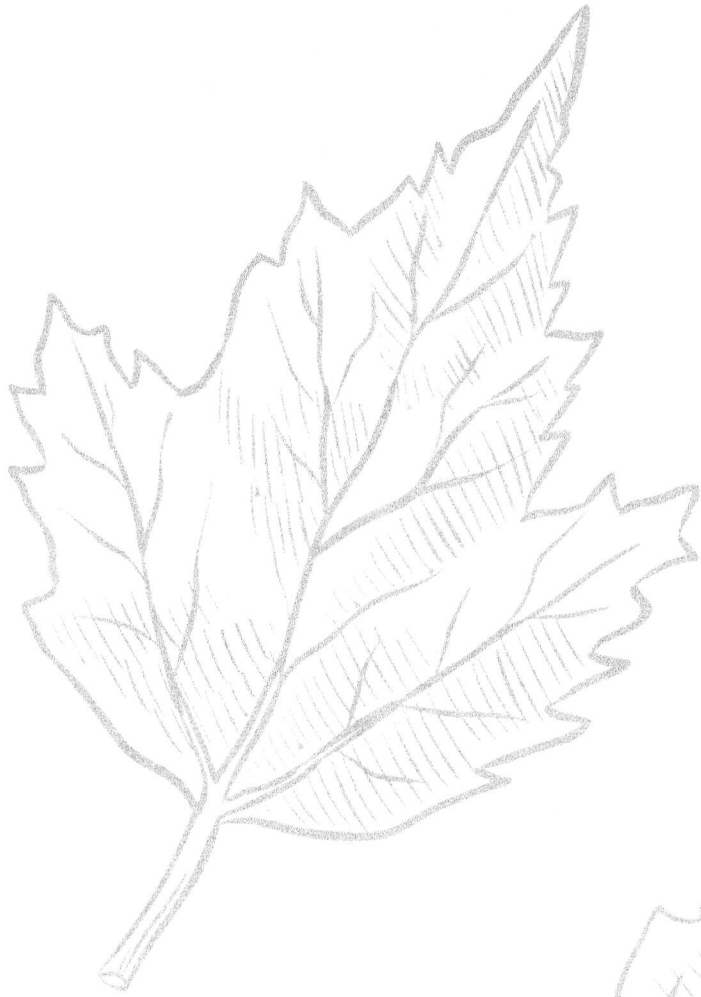

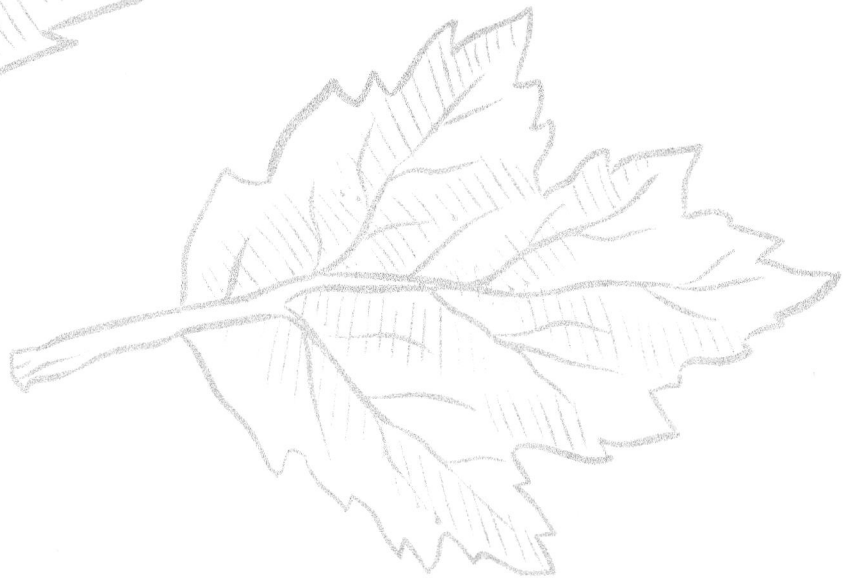

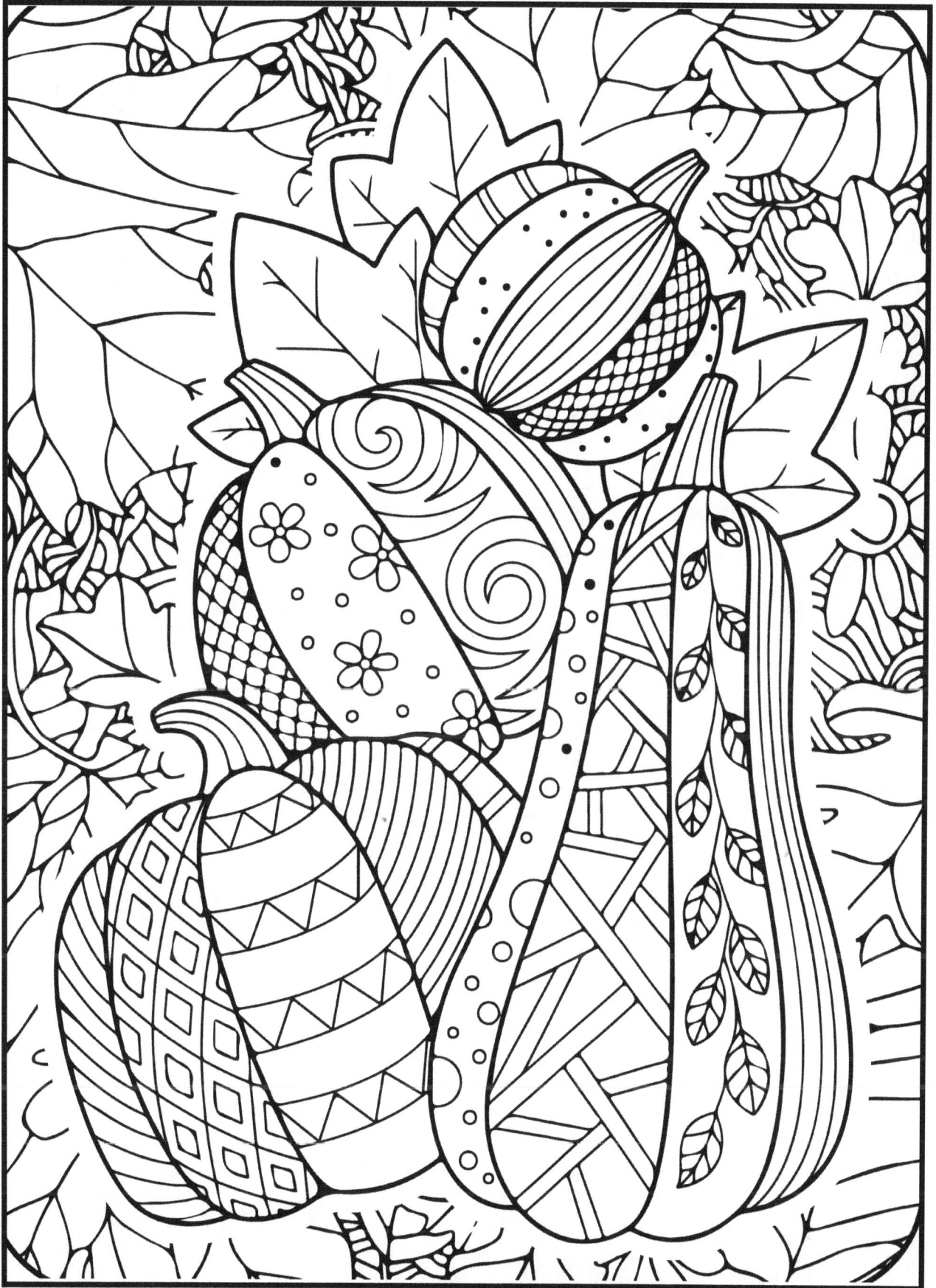

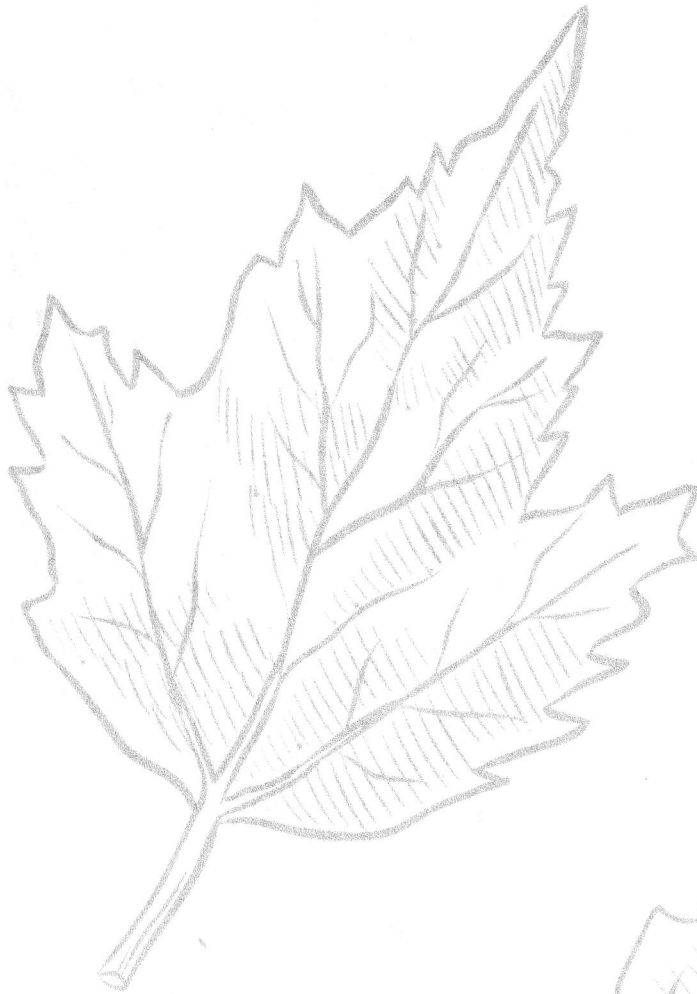

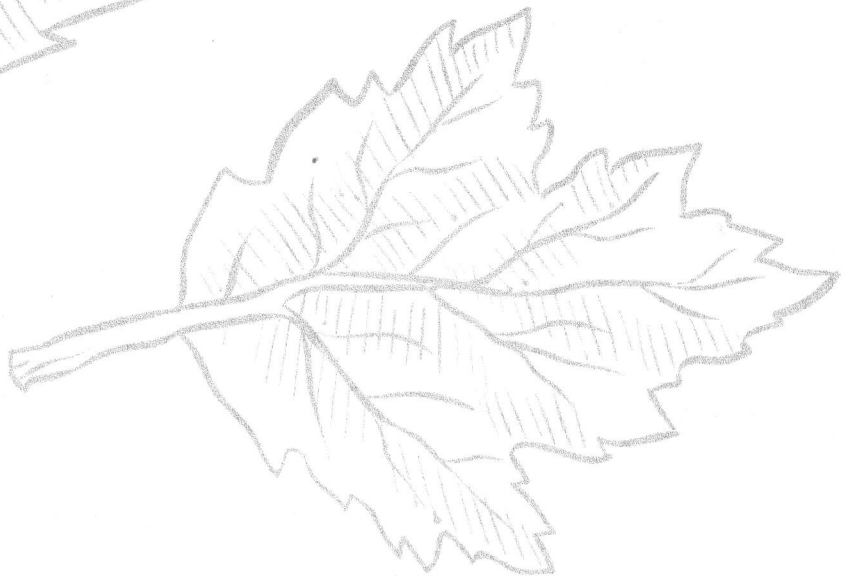